Second Edition

The Pitman Guide to

English Language Examinations

Susan Davies
Richard West

Pitman

PITMAN PUBLISHING LIMITED
128 Long Acre, London WC2E 9AN

Associated Companies
Pitman Publishing Pty Ltd, Melbourne
Pitman Publishing New Zealand Ltd, Wellington

First published in Great Britain 1981
Second edition 1984

British Library Cataloguing in Publication Data

Davies, Susan
The Pitman guide to English language examinations.—
2nd ed.
1. English Language—Textbooks for foreign speakers
I. Title II. West, Richard
428.2'4 PE1128

ISBN 0 273 02035 8

Text set in 10 on 12pt Ehrhardt Roman
Printed and bound in Great Britain at The Pitman Press, Bath

Contents

Appendices

Introduction to the first edition

This Guide is intended to be of use to students whose mother tongue is not English, to teachers, to schools and colleges and to employers.

The examinations which have been included have been chosen because they are predominantly UK-based English language examinations widely taken by non-native speakers. There are 3 types of examination described:

a Examinations in English as a foreign language specifically designed for non-native speakers.
b Examinations in English language designed for native speakers but taken widely by non-native speakers (excluding those taken in state schools, ie GCE and CSE examinations).
c Special purpose examinations, particularly those in commercial or scientific/technical English.

A number of examinations have been excluded because they are outside the scope of the Guide, ie those not taken widely by non-native speakers, those developed for specific purposes within institutes and those which are not UK-based. The examinations are presented in alphabetical order; thus the order is no reflection of the relative merits of each examination.

Each examination is described in a uniform way as follows:

A **Title** The full name of the examination (abbreviation in brackets).
B **Conducted by** The examining body with its address and telephone number. Any affiliations to the examining body are mentioned here.
C **Status** Details of whether the examination is recognized by an outside body, whether it is part of another qualification or can stand on its own.
D **Aims** Details of the aims of each examination, and whether it assesses a candidate's knowledge of general English or English for a specific purpose (ESP).
E **Level** Levels are related approximately to the standards of GCE, CSE and the examinations of the Cambridge Syndicate. Compara-

tive levels of different examinations are given in the tables in Appendices 1 and 2.

F **Availability** Details of when, where and to whom each examination is available.

G **Content** A summary of the content of each examination is given with specimen questions. The time allocated to the examination and to individual questions as well as to the marks allocated are given where appropriate.

H **Results** Details are given on how the results are graded, what constitutes a pass and whether a pass counts towards a further qualification. An outline of group certificate schemes in commercial education is given in the table in Appendix 3.

I **Further information** Here are listed the information and publications available from examining bodies. Details of prices and postage rates should be obtained from the examining bodies.

Other information contained in the Guide is:

a A multilingual explanation of the headings used in the description of each examination (A to I above). This will be of particular use to institutes overseas and students coming to the United Kingdom to further their education.

b A summary of the most widely-used examinations for teachers of EFL (Appendix 4).

c An appendix listing the names and addresses of various professional institutes setting English language or Communication papers as part of their examinations for membership or associateship (Appendix 5).

d An appendix listing the names and addresses of various overseas examinations councils (Appendix 6).

e Finally, there is a Glossary defining the terms used in the descriptions of the examinations which have special meaning in the context of language testing.

The Pitman Guide to English Language Examinations has been designed so that it can be revised simply and regularly to keep pace with syllabus changes and the introduction of new examinations.

Susan Davies & Richard West
1981

Introduction to the second edition

The 1970s were a period of great innovation in foreign language teaching – one thinks particularly of the work of the Council of Europe (developing notional/functional syllabuses, preparing the Waystage and Threshold syllabus specifications, and introducing the idea of unit/credit examinations), the trend towards more 'communicative' approaches to language learning, and the emergence of English for specific purposes (ESP). Innovations in language examinations inevitably lag behind developments in teaching, but by 1981, when the first edition of *The Pitman Guide to English Language Examinations* was published, many of these trends were being reflected in new English language examinations.

In the three years since the publication of the first edition these trends have become firmly established, with the introduction of new examinations and the extensive revision of most existing ones. The result is that this second edition has had to be completely revised and expanded to take account of these developments. Nearly all examining boards now recognize that English is a language to be used for international communication rather than simply a system of grammatical rules, and, with the introduction of the new Institute of Linguists' EFL examinations, we see the first papers geared to Council of Europe levels. There has also been an increase in the number of ESP examinations, especially those designed for students following occupational or vocational courses.

In order to chart the developments in EFL/ESL examinations in the last decade, we have drawn up ten questions, each with two possible answers – type *a* and type *b*. An examination designed in the late sixties would produce type *a* responses to each question, while an examination of the eighties will be more likely to bring a string of type *b* responses. In this way it is possible to trace the developments in English language examining in general, or to assess any one examination in particular.

1 What apparently is the underlying aim of language learning?

a The acquisition of linguistic (ie grammatical) competence.

b The acquisition of communicative competence (ie the ability to use the language for effective communication).

2 What is the basic approach to language testing?

a Synthetic, ie a language is composed of the sum of its parts and we can test knowledge of the whole by sampling knowledge of the parts.

b Analytic, ie communication involves more than the assembly of isolated parts and we should test the ability to combine the parts effectively.

3 What type of language knowledge is to be tested predominantly?

a Usage, ie accurate knowledge of the grammatical rules of the language.

b Use, ie the ability to use the language to communicate fluently.

4 What types of question are used principally?

a Discrete point, eg a battery of multiple-choice questions each testing a single language point.

b Global, eg free-response questions drawing on a range of language skills.

5 What types of texts and tasks are used in the questions?

a Idealized texts specially produced for the examination; unrealistic tasks not required of candidates outside the examination hall.

b Authentic texts not designed for examination purposes; realistic tasks such as those required of candidates in the real world.

6 What range of skills is tested?

a Narrow, concentrating on the receptive skills of reading and listening.

b A full range, including the productive skills of speaking and writing.

7 How much attention is paid to contextualization?

a Very little; sufficient only to indicate the response required.

b Full context supplied in the belief that meaning is derived from linguistic and situational context.

8 What is the primary purpose of English language examining?

a Attainment testing designed to measure and compare the amount of language candidates have accurately mastered.

Therefore examinations should be primarily norm-referenced.

b Proficiency testing designed to assess whether candidates will be able to perform the language tasks required of them. Therefore examinations will be primarily criterion-referenced.

9 What is the main criterion of a 'good examination'?

a Reliability, ie it is statistically consistent from centre to centre, year to year.

b Validity, ie it tests and can be seen to test relevant language skills.

10 What range of candidates should an examination be suitable for?

a Broad, ie covering a wide range of candidates with a single examination.

b Narrow, ie the examination is designed for a more specific audience whose language aims can be identified more precisely (although related papers may be available at other levels or in different skills).

Other developments in EFL/ESL examinations in the past decade relate to practicalities rather than content or format. These developments include the more frequent availability of examinations – increasingly, papers are available several times a year or even, in the case of PEI, available on demand. Secondly, an extension of the ESP approach is the so-called 'mode 3' system now available from the RSA, under which examination papers can be set at specified levels but to reflect the individual syllabuses of particular schools or groups of learners. Thirdly, there has been an expansion of the unit/credit idea proposed by the Council of Europe, allowing candidates to be given credit for parts (units) of an examination taken successfully without having to resit the whole examination at a later date.

We should like to thank everyone who has commented on the first edition and encouraged us to produce a second.

Susan Davies and Richard West
1984

Acknowledgments

We wish to acknowledge the help and advice received from the examining bodies who approved the relevant summaries of examinations included in this Guide, and to thank them for permission to use copyright material which is included in the main specimen questions.

Examination Summaries

Explanation of the headings used in the description of each examination

Title	Titel	Tlτλος	Título	Titre	Titulo	اسم الامتحان	A
Conducted by	Durchgeführt von	Διεξάγεται ὑπό	Dirigido por	Dirigé par	Conduzidos	الهيئة المشرفة عليه	B
Status	Wertbemessung	'Αξιολόγηση	Grado	Statut	Posicão	أهميته	C
Aims	Ziele	Σκοπol	Objetos	Buts	Objectivos	أهدافه	D
Level	Niveau	'Επlπεδο	Nivel	Niveau	Nivel	مستواه	E
Availability	Zulassung	Διαθεσιμότης	Habilitación	Disponibilité	Disponibilidade	إمكانية التقديم الى هذا الامتحان	F
Content	Umfang	Πεςιεχόμενο	Contenido	Contenu	Contento	تفاصيل الامتحان	G
Results	Ergebnisse	'Αποτελέσματα	Resultados	Résultats	Resultados	الدرجات المطلوبه	H
Further information	Weitere Einzelheiten	Περαιτέρω Πληροφορlες	Información adicional	Renseignements obtenus après enquête	Informação addicional	معلومات اضافيه	I

1 Associated Examining Board (AEB)

1.1 English language – professional and business use

Title

Conducted by
The Associated Examining Board (AEB)
Wellington House, Aldershot, Hampshire GU11 1BQ
Tel: Aldershot (0252) 25551

Status
A single-subject GCE O level examination.

Aims
An examination designed for English mother-tongue students in sixth forms and in further education who plan to enter the professions or to follow a career in business or commerce.

Level
A GCE Ordinary (Alternative) level examination set at a level somewhat beyond GCE O level English Language papers.

Availability
Available only through educational establishments registered as AEB examination centres. Examinations are held once a year in June. Centres wishing to enter candidates for this examination must inform AEB not later than 16 October the preceding year.

Content

Paper 1 (2 hours)

Marks

1 **Composition** A composition of a minimum length of 400 words on one topic from a choice of 7. Topics are related to candidates' background, experience and proposed career. — 50

Examples
a Television commercials
b Should strikes be made illegal?

2 **Summary** An exercise requiring the use of summarizing techniques on a passage of prose approximately 600 words in length. — 30

Paper 2 (2 hours)

1 **Reading comprehension** 8–10 free-response questions — 40

testing understanding of the ideas and language in a prose passage of not more than 600 words.

2 **Composition** 2 questions chosen from the following:

a Letter-writing 20

Writing a letter or a sequence of letters to fit a given situation.

Example

You are a member of the Committee of a Sports Club (choose your own sport). At its last meeting, your Committee was disappointed at the way the sport was developing in the area and felt that it would be useful to host a one-day meeting of representatives of all other clubs in the area to discuss the situation. You have been asked to draft a circular letter to be sent to the secretaries of these clubs. In it you should explain why you feel the meeting is necessary and what it hopes to achieve. Give full information of the date, time and place. You should also draft an appropriate reply slip, to be included with the letter.

b Factual writing 20

The drafting of a short report, a memorandum, an advertisement, a notice or a questionnaire from material supplied.

Example

Your school/college recently held a dance at which there was a small fire caused by an electrical fault on the hired equipment. One of those present also received burns to her right hand, though fortunately no one else was hurt. The Head/Principal has called for a full report to be put to the Governors. As Secretary of the Dance Committee you are required to write the report; add any further details which you consider important.

c The interpretation of statistics or graphic material. 20

Paper 3 (10–15 minutes)

A test of spoken English conducted internally.

1 **Oral report** A report on a prepared topic delivered from notes. 20

2 **Discussion, interview or telephone conversation** An exchange of information and ideas with one other person. 20

Results Papers are graded at 5 levels of pass – A, B, C, D and E – and U (unclassified).

Further information Available from AEB: Syllabuses, Section II: past papers; reports of examiners, Section 2, for recent years; *How examination papers are set and marked*; *Criteria and assessment in English*; *Notes for guidance on the assessment of the spoken English component.*

1.2 Test in English for educational purposes (TEEP)

Title

Conducted by

The Associated Examining Board (AEB)
Wellington House, Aldershot, Hampshire GU11 1BQ
Tel: Aldershot (0252) 25551

Status

An examination for overseas students applying for admission to institutions of further and higher education in the United Kingdom.

Aims

The examination assesses a candidate's ability:

a to produce adequate written English for formal academic writing tasks
b to understand spoken English for listening to lectures and discussions
c to understand written English for reading textbooks and other sources of information both intensively and extensively
d to produce adequate spoken English for taking part in an academic discussion and presenting papers

Level

The examination is designed for students considering embarking on academic courses ranging from GCE A level to university postgraduate level.

Availability

Available at AEB-approved centres, initially in the UK only. Examinations are held 3 times a year, in January, May and September. Open to non-native speakers of English from the UK or overseas.

Content

The examination is held in 3 sessions:

Session I

Part 1 **Reading ability** (1¼ hours)

Candidates have to complete 2 tasks:

a To write a summary of parts of a passage, assisted by brief notes taken during reading.
b To write short answers to a number of questions on the same passage.

Part 2 **Ability to understand spoken English** (10 minutes)

Candidates hear a dictation recording once only. During pauses in the recording, they have to write down what the speaker has said.

Part 3 **Ability to understand spoken English** (50 minutes)

a Candidates hear a tape recording of a short lecture once only and have to take notes with the aid of a printed framework of questions and statements. After the lecture, they have to use the notes to write answers to the questions based on the lecture.

b Candidates have to write a summary of parts of the lecture, using the lecture outline provided and their own notes.

Session II

Part 1 Reading ability (50 minutes)

Candidates have to complete 2 tasks based on 2 different reading passages:

a Establishing where words are missing from a passage and writing these words in spaces provided.

b Writing short answers to a number of questions based on a second passage.

Part 2 Ability to understand spoken English (30 minutes)

Candidates hear a tape recording of a short interview once only and have to take notes with the aid of a printed framework of questions. After the interview, they have to use the notes to write answers to the questions on the interview.

Part 3 Ability to write English (65 minutes)

a Writing a summary using notes made on the second passage in Part 1 and relevant information from Part 2.

b Rewriting a short passage which contains a number of errors, making all the necessary corrections.

Session III

Ability to speak in English

a Candidates have to speak about themselves for one minute.

b Candidates have to respond to a number of remarks that might be made to them, or to situations they might find themselves in when they are in Britain.

c Candidates have to listen to a discussion and at certain points they have to answer questions or give their opinions.

d Candidates have a specific task to complete which involves asking questions relating to non-verbal information, eg charts, diagrams, graphs, etc.

e Candidates are given a printed passage and have 5 minutes in which to prepare an answer to a question set on this material. They then have 2 minutes to present their answer.

Results

AEB provides a profile of the candidate's proficiency in reading, listening, writing and speaking. The profile is intended *a* to show receiving institutions how well a student might be expected to cope with the situations in an academic environment and *b* to show those areas in which students might need help.

Further information

Further information on the development of the project and the introduction of the examination can be obtained from:

Mr A M Emmett, Assistant Secretary
The Associated Examining Board
Wellington House, Aldershot, Hampshire GU11 1BQ

2 Association of Recognized English Language Schools Examinations Trust (AET)

Title

2.1 ARELS oral examinations
Preliminary AP series (Preliminary/Waystage)
Higher certificate AH series (Intermediate)
Diploma AD series (Advanced)

Conducted by Association of Recognized English Language Schools Examinations Trust (AET)
113 Banbury Road, Oxford OX2 6JX
Tel: Oxford (0865) 514272 Telex: 83147 *attn* AET

Status Single-subject examinations, unique in that they are designed for use in language laboratories.

Aims To provide comprehensive, valid and reliable assessments of ability in the use and comprehension of spoken English at 3 levels.

Levels **Preliminary** The oral counterpart of the Preliminary Examination in English as a Foreign Language (written English) of the University of Oxford Delegacy's Examinations (see **13.1**).

This level is appropriate for someone who has picked up English in the course of work or travel. He/she may often need the speaker to repeat what has been said, and may have to think carefully before talking, but given time to do this, they can express ordinary needs.

Higher Certificate The oral counterpart of the Higher Level Examination in English as a Foreign Language (written English) of the University of Oxford Delegacy's Examinations (see **13.1**).

This level is suitable for someone who can communicate and understand effectively, who can manage in everyday situations in an English-speaking environment quite well, although with occasional difficulties. More complex situations would still prove troublesome most of the time.

Diploma Demands a mastery of everyday English, but tests in addition the use of English as a medium of abstract and intellectual thought and its use in situations more demanding than those normally encountered in everyday life.

For comparative levels of EFL examinations, see Appendix 1.

Candidates can enrol for the examination: **Availability**

a through any language school in the UK if taking a course there
b through one of the accredited examination centres in another country
c by direct application to the ARELS Examinations Trust

Higher Certificate candidates should be at least 16. Diploma candidates must be at least 18. There is no minimum age for the Preliminary examination.

A timetable for examinations is available through the Trust. Local Trust Administrators have authority to vary the dates slightly and if numbers require, to set the examination on more than one date. For schools whose course dates do not fit the set examining dates, the 'Opportunity Examining' scheme allows candidates to be entered on other dates. Details are available through the Trust.

All the examinations are designed to be conducted in language laboratory booths. Candidates' responses are recorded for marking. **Content**

Preliminary (Approximately 30 minutes)

The examination tests competence in 3 areas:

1 **Social English** Candidates must be able to:

a Read and write numbers, letters and common abbreviations.

Example
Candidates hear:

His car number is JYK 766G. That's JYK 766G.

On the answer sheet they must complete:

His car number is [ ]

b Participate in short, simple cued conversation, possibly using visual stimuli.

Example
Candidates hear the following to which they must speak their answers. The time allowed for response is given in brackets. The response time is not given to candidates, but appears on the console operator's script.

Where do you come from? (5 seconds)
Ah, yes. What's your capital city called? (5 seconds)
How did you come to England? (8 seconds)

c Respond appropriately to everyday situations described simply.

Example
Candidates hear:

You see some sunglasses in a shop. You want to know the price. What do you say? (12 seconds)

d Answer questions in directed situations.

Example
Candidates hear a question and must speak their answer:
How do you want your coffee? (8 seconds)
Do you mind if I smoke? (8 seconds)

2 Comprehension Candidates must be able to:

a Understand the exact meaning of a simple piece of speech and show this by:

1 marking a map, plan or grid

Example
On their answer sheets candidates have a map. They listen to the following and then have to mark the Post Office.

A: Excuse me, can you tell me where I can find a post office?
B: Certainly. This is Taylor Road. You go straight up here to the crossroads. Then you turn left along Charles Street and there's one on the corner, just opposite the park.
A: Sorry, can you repeat that? (The directions are repeated.)

2 choosing the most appropriate set of visuals

Example
In their answer books, candidates have four pictures. They hear a description of one of the pictures and they must choose the correct picture.

It's got tables and chairs outside and a big menu near the door. You'll see people sitting outside.

Candidates see a picture of a cafe without a menu but with people sitting outside, one of a cafe with a menu but no people sitting outside, one of a cafe with a menu and one person sitting outside and a cafe as described on the tape.

3 stating whether or not, or how, the social stimulus relates to a visual

Example
In their answer books, candidates have a picture of a hotel room with several things wrong with it. They must tell a travel agent about the room. Before answering they hear the following:

Your hotel room is not very good. It's noisy, there's nowhere for your clothes, the window does not work, there's no hot water.

4 answering simple questions
The candidates hear a conversation twice. The conversation is deliberately imperfect, reflecting spoken rather than written

English. The second hearing is interrupted by questions and candidates must speak their answers.

Example

Interviewer	Well, Mike, and can you tell me, how did you start in the music business?
Mike	Well, my family were very musical, and I studied the piano and then I studied the guitar.
Interviewer	I see, well, this was when you were young.

When did he start to play music? (10 seconds)

b Understand the basic and essential meaning of a piece of speech too difficult to be understood completely

Example
Candidates listen to the following and mark the best answer in their answer books.

Police are looking for thieves who broke into a house in Hertfordshire and stole an oil painting valued at £2000. The painting by the Dutch artist Jan Lief Pietschoof shows a large ship entering a harbour. It's 18 inches by 24 inches and was painted between 1652 and 1719.
This is about

☐	a ship in a harbour
☐	a stolen painting
☐	police problems at ports

3 **Extended speaking** Candidates are required to speak for 45–60 seconds in situations likely to be appropriate in real life for a speaker at this level. This may include explanation, advice, requests, apologies, etc but will not demand any use of the language in other than mundane and pressing circumstances.

Higher Certificate (about 35 minutes) **& Diploma** (about 45 minutes)

Both examinations follow a similar format, testing 6 major skills:

1 **Social responses** This tests the use of language in common situations.

Examples
Candidates have to reply to questions or remarks:

Shouldn't you be wearing something warmer? (6 seconds)

and are given situations:

It is late in the evening and you suddenly start to get toothache. Ask a friend for help and advice.

2 Intelligible speech This tests intonation, stress, rhythm and pronunciation.

Example

Candidates have a dialogue written in their answer sheets. They have 2 minutes to study the passage, and then must read aloud the part marked *Candidate*.

John: 86431
Candidate: Ah, hello John. You fly quite a bit, don't you?
John: Yes.
Candidate: Good. I thought you did. I never have you know, but now I've got that job as an English teacher in Manila I've got to fly out there. I've just picked up my ticket. Some of the conditions are a bit disconcerting – to a first-timer at any rate.

etc.

3 Audial comprehension This tests comprehension of a fairly long piece of speech. The passage is played through twice, the second time interrupted by questions. Candidates must speak their answers.

4 Sustained speaking At Higher Certificate level, candidates hear a text and have a series of pictures to use in telling a story. At Diploma level a piece of natural speech is played twice from which candidates must give an oral summary.

5 Oral accuracy This tests grammar. Candidates hear a sentence which they have to change or respond to when given a cue or pattern to follow.

Examples

Cue: I'm angry. *Response*: What are you angry about?
I'm frightened.
I'm clever. etc

Cue: I could have eaten a horse. *Response*: Yes, I was hungry too.
My hair was standing on end.
I was absolutely whacked.

6 Free oral expression A list of 5 topics is given to candidates 20 minutes before the examination and candidates choose one. At Higher Certificate level, there is one minute to talk on the chosen topic and $1\frac{1}{2}$ minutes at Diploma level.

Examples of topics

Higher Certificate

Travelling is the best form of education.
Three years is long enough for anyone to spend at university.

Diploma

In modern society, privacy is becoming a thing of the past.
Why I'm not interested in the news.

Results Results are published in 3 ways, one of them optional at extra cost:

a Each candidate receives a result slip which states the grade awarded.

In the Preliminary examination there are 3 grades of pass and 2 of failure. In the Higher Certificate and Diploma there are 7 grades of pass and 3 of failure.

b Successful candidates receive a Certificate or Diploma, recording one of 3 grades of pass.

c (Optional on payment of a fee.) Details of all the marks gained by candidates in the sections of the examinations. Thus, for example, a Diploma examination, having 6 sections, each of them marked at least twice, would generate at least 12 section marks as well as subjective impression, totals and final results. This service enables the examinations to be used for diagnostic purposes.

Further information

A list of publications, regulations, tapes, past examinations and books may be obtained from the Trust. The following are provided free: *Rationale, Development and Methods, A Guide for Examination Centres* and *Single Keys of Recent Examinations.*

3 British Council/University of Cambridge Local Examinations Syndicate

Title

3.1 English language testing service

Conducted by The British Council
10 Spring Gardens, London SW1A 2BN
Tel: London (01) 930 8466
and
University of Cambridge Local Examinations Syndicate
Syndicate Buildings, 1 Hills Road, Cambridge CB1 2EU
Tel: Cambridge (0223) 61111

Status An English Language test recognized by governmental, academic and professional bodies in the UK for admission purposes.

Aims To assess to what extent the English language ability of candidates will enable them to meet the demands of a course of study in an English-medium educational institution. To provide a profile of the language performance of each candidate which can be compared with that required for the course of study which he/she wishes to pursue.

Levels A profile of each candidate's performance is producd according to a system of language mastery bands. These bands range from very low levels of performance (Bands 1 and 2) to extremely effective levels (Bands 8 and 9). The band descriptions are shown in the accompanying table. See Appendix 2 for comparative levels of ESP examinations.

Availability The Service is available in British Council centres throughout the world and in regional centres in the UK. When entering for the Test candidates must choose an appropriate Module according to their field of study. Modules are available in 5 ESP fields (Life Sciences, Medicine, Physical Sciences, Social Studies and Technology). In addition there is an interdisciplinary General Academic Module. A Non-Academic Training Module, introduced in 1983, caters for technical/vocational trainees.

Content Candidates may choose to take the Academic or Non-Academic modules.

Band	Descriptors
9	**Expert user** Fully operational command of the language; appropriate, accurate and fluent with complete understanding.
8	**Very good user** Fully operational command of the language; occasional minor inaccuracies, inappropriacies or misunderstandings possible in unfamiliar situations.
7	**Good user** Operational command of the language; occasional inaccuracies, inappropriacies and misunderstandings in some situations.
6	**Competent user** Generally effective command of the language, although occasional misunderstanding and lack of fluency could interfere with communication.
5	**Modest user** Partial command of the language coping with overall meaning in most situations, although some misunderstanding and lack of fluency could block communication.
4	**Limited user** Basic functional competence limited to familiar situations, but frequent problems in understanding and fluency can make communication a constant effort.
3	**Extremely limited user** Below level of functional competence; although general meaning can be conveyed and understood in simple situations, there are repeated breakdowns in communication.
2	**Intermittent user** No real communication possible although single-word messages may be conveyed and understood.
1	**Non-user** Unable to use the language or does not provide relevant evidence of language competence for assessment.

1 Academic modules

The test is made up of 2 sections, a General Section sampling general features of use of the language in communication (2 sub-tests) and a Modular (ESP) Section related to specific fields of study (3 sub-tests).

General section

G1 Reading Comprehension (40 minutes)

Candidates are provided with a question booklet. All questions are multiple choice, eg:

Matching sentences Candidates must choose from among 4 the sentence that could best replace the original one.

Example
There isn't enough sugar in the tea.

A The tea isn't sweet enough.
B There isn't much sugar in the tea.
C There's too little sugar in the tea.
D There's no sugar in the tea.

Cloze passage A prose passage of approximately 500 words from which certain words have been deleted. Candidates must choose from among four the best word to fill the gap.

Parallel texts A number of short passages all dealing with the same subject but containing different viewpoints and/or manners of writing. The questions test understanding of each passage in itself and the candidate's ability to make comparisons and cross-references between them.

G2 Listening Comprehension (30 minutes)

Texts and instructions are recorded on a tape cassette, candidates are provided with a question booklet. All questions are multiple choice, eg:

Choosing from diagrams A series of spoken descriptions involving spatial, dimensional, graphical etc, conventions which candidates must match up with printed diagrams or figures.

Example
You hear:

'Which shape consists of a square with a circle inside it?'

Four figures are given. Look at them and choose the one you think answers the question best.

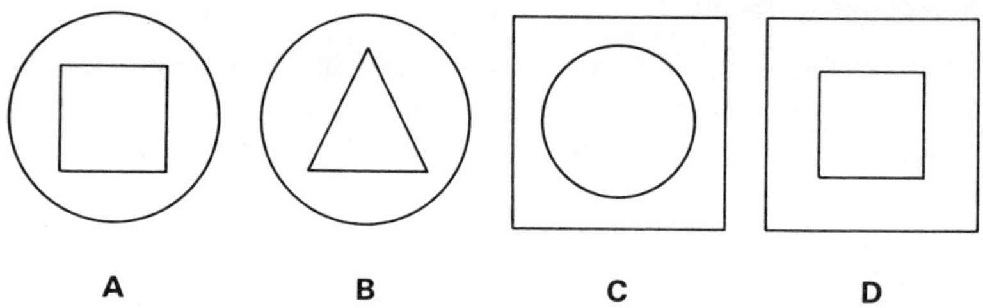

Listening to an interview Extracts from an interview or discussion between two people. Questions test a candidate's understanding of what is heard.

Replying to questions A series of questions to which candidates must choose the most appropriate reply.

Example
You hear:

What are you doing now?

Four replies are given. Read them and choose the one which you think is best.

A I'm going there next week.
B It's a very large dog.
C Yes indeed.
D I'm looking for my passport.

Listening to a seminar An extract from a seminar. Questions test memory of salient points, comments, information, inferences, etc, figuring in the cross-talk.

Modular section

At the time of the examination candidates are provided with an appropriate Source Booklet containing authentic texts from their specialist fields, which form the basis of all the tests in this Section.

M1 Study Skills (55 minutes)

Candidates are provided with the appropriate Question Booklet. Multiple-choice questions test the candidate's control of the language skills used when studying particular specialist fields.

Examples of questions based on particular texts

Life Sciences
Read the text *Agar Medium* (*for slides*) and then answer the questions below:

Which one of the 4 sequences of activities shown below is correct for the preparation of Agar Medium to be stored before use?

Activities
1 Bring pressure to 15 lb per in.
2 Allow to cool.
3 Add yeast extract, boric acid and sucrose to cold water.
4 Stir in 1 g powdered Agar.
5 Place bottle of Agar mixture in autoclave.
6 Continue heating for 15 min.

A	3	5	4	1	6	2
B	3	4	5	6	1	2
C	4	3	5	6	1	2
D	3	4	5	1	6	2

Medicine
Read the text *Euthanasia* and then answer the questions below:

Which of the following, according to the survey, agree that some patients should be allowed to die without great efforts being made to prolong their lives?

A College students
B Senior students
C First-year medical students
D First-year nursing students

Physical Sciences
Read the text *Absolute Zero* and then answer these questions:

This passage suggests that absolute zero can, theoretically, be achieved by

A only a gas
B only an ideal gas
C all forms of matter
D all forms of energy

Technology
Read the text *The Heat Pump* and then answer these questions:

The best title for the diagram at the foot of the page is

A Efficiency of the pump
B Operation of the heat pump
C Mechanism of the heat pump
D Installation of the heat pump

General Academic
Read the text *Education and Society* and then answer these questions:

The last sentence of the second paragraph serves as

A a summary
B an illustration
C an explanation
D a counter argument

M2 Writing (40 minutes)

Two tasks aimed at assessing a candidate's ability to present written information in his/her own or a related field.

1 A directed essay developing out of a topic or theme figuring in the Source Booklet.

Examples

Life Sciences
Refer to *Problems in Mechanized Co-operative Farming* in your Source Booklet. Write 15–20 lines suggesting ways in which some of the handicaps mentioned might be overcome.

Social Studies
Refer to *The Delinquent Way of Life* in your Source Booklet. To what extent do you think imprisonment is a real deterrent to crime? Write 15–20 lines.

Technology
Refer to *The Digital Road to Better Records* in your Source Booklet. Taking any technological development of the past 50 years, illustrate how this has improved living in your own country. Write 15–20 lines.

Physical Sciences
Refer to *The Call for an Index of Risks* in your Source Booklet. Discuss, in 15–20 lines, the type and importance of safety procedures you think should be present in a science laboratory.

Medicine
Refer to *Procedures in ante- and post-natal care* in your Source Booklet. Write 15–20 lines describing what, in your opinion, are the advantages of women having their confinements at home rather than in a hospital.

General Academic
Refer to *Etymological Confusion* in your Source Booklet. Discuss in 15–20 lines the advantages or the disadvantages of using English as the medium of study in your own profession or area of interest.

2 A task involving the extraction and manipulation of data, inferences or ideas from a specific part of a text in the Source Booklet.

Examples

Life Sciences
Refer to *The Basis of Ecology* in your Source Booklet. Show how Figure 1 illustrates the fundamental food-providing relationships that may be expected in any ecosystem.

Technology
Refer to *Icebergs are a Frozen Asset* in your Source Booklet. Drawing information from the diagram on page 13, describe how it might be possible to tap the freshwater potential of polar regions.

Medicine
Refer to *Non-fatal injuries sustained by seat-belt wearers* in your Source Booklet. From a careful study of Figures 1 and 2 suggest in what ways the compulsory use of seat-belts might change the pattern of injuries in road-traffic accidents.

Social Studies
Refer to *Prospect Facing Youth* in your Source Booklet. What does Table 1 tell you about the changing picture of youth unemployment over the last 10 years of the period under review?

Physical Sciences
Refer to *Chemical Effects of Electric Current* in your Source Booklet. To what extent do the contents of page 9 offer a good example of the way in which a laboratory experiment should be written up?

General Academic
Refer to *The 15th Century Twilight* in your Source Booklet. Describe how, according to the writer, historians in the 19th century viewed the Wars of the Roses.

M3 Interview (about 10 minutes)

This is structured in 3 phrases:

Phase 1 Simple, straightforward exchanges on personal/professional data, family, weather, home region, knowledge of the UK, etc.
Phase 2 A discussion devoted to a particular topic or piece of a text from the Source Booklet. Questions are based on data (tabulated, graphical or diagrammatic), illustration or general topics and test the candidate's skills of describing, comparing, inferring and identifying.
Phase 3 Candidates are asked to speak at length, for example on their study plans, how they think UK training would benefit them, etc.

2 Non-Academic Module

The Non-Academic Training Module consists of 3 sub-tests, and contains texts and tasks appropriate to practical, technical training.

M1 Listening test (30 minutes)

Text and instructions are recorded on a tape cassette. Candidates are provided with a question booklet. All sections are multiple choice questions.

M2 Reading and writing test (45 minutes)

Mostly multiple choice questions, but one writing task.

M3 Interview (10-15 minutes)

This is structured in 2 phases:

a Discussion of a process.
b Candidates are asked to speak at greater length on their work, their training plans, etc.

Results A Test Report Form is completed for each candidate and despatched to the educational institution(s) or training organization(s) the candidate wishes to enter. It shows the Overall (average) Band awarded and a profile of the individual Band scores obtained in the component parts of the Test. Where a candidate's Band score indicates that the language performance is inadequate to enter a course of further education, guidance is given as to the number of hours' tuition required to reach the appropriate level.

Further information Available from the British Council or the University of Cambridge Local Examinations Syndicate: *English Language Testing Service – User Handbook* and *English Language Testing Service – Annual Report.*

4 City and Guilds of London Institute

4.1 Communication in technical English

Title

Conducted by
City and Guilds of London Institute
46 Britannia Street, London WC1X 9RG
Tel: London (01) 278 2468

Status
Single subject examination.

Aims
To provide a scheme and examination in technical English for students whose first language is not necessarily English so that they:

a may meet more effectively with the requirements of their employment
b may meet with the demands of any technical course they are following
c may prepare themselves for further study or promotion opportunities

Level
An elementary examination set at a level approximately equivalent to the lower grades of GCE O level or CSE.

Availability
Candidates may enter either as internal candidates, who at the time of entry are undertaking (or have already completed) an approved course at a technical college or other establishment, or as external candidates. Permission is *not* required from the Institute, but candidates must submit their entries through an approved examination centre.

Content
There are 2 papers:

Paper 1 Understanding (2 hours)

There are 5 compulsory questions based on the simple interpretation of items selected from a variety of written and graphical information, including items from:

Textbooks, handbooks, instruction manuals and schedules, technical journals, labels, directions, notices, forms, questionnaires, worksheets, payslips, memoranda, requests, messages, letters of application, complaints, enquiries, orders for items, reports, safety procedures, setting up/assembly of equipment, demonstrations, sketches, simple plans and diagrams, exploded drawings, pie charts, simple graphs, histograms and pictograms, handouts, worksheets, invoices and question papers, reference sources including dictionaries, British Standards, year books, manuals, directories and catalogues.

Example
In the 4 columns set out below there are 5 words or phrases that are in some way related to the work of a *motor mechanic*, 5 to that of a *cook*, 5 to that of a *builder*, 5 to that of a *printer*. Many of the words are in the wrong column. Rearrange them all correctly in 4 columns headed: *Motor mechanic, Cook, Builder, Printer.*

poaching	freezer	alternator	proteins	
monotype	anti-freeze	whisk	rolling pin	
timing	distributor	fly-leaf	tenon	
plane	spirit level	shuttering	graphics	
engraving	platemaking	grease gun	pincers	(20 marks)

Paper II Writing (2 hours)

There are 5 compulsory questions in which candidates are expected to communicate explicitly and appropriately in written and graphical form. The emphasis is on realistic situations.

Example
A vehicle manufacturer produces 3 products: cars, vans and trucks. At the end of the year, the company shows that $\frac{1}{3}$ of its profits are made on the cars, $\frac{1}{6}$ on the vans and the rest on the trucks. Construct a pie chart to illustrate the company's profits. (10 marks)

Results The criterion of successful performance in this examination is that of communicative competence, appropriate to technical experience. Successful candidates receive a Certificate in Communication in Technical English. Each candidate receives a grade for each paper. There are 4 grades: Distinction, Credit, Pass and Fail. Certificates are awarded for a pass in both papers. Candidates who were successful in one paper but not in both may carry forward their success and need subsequently retake only the one paper in which they were unsuccessful.

Further information A syllabus and specimen papers are available from the Sales Section of the City and Guilds of London Institute, 76 Portland Place, London W1N 4AA.

5 Educational Testing Service

Title

5.1 Test of English as a Foreign Language (TOEFL)

Conducted by

Educational Testing Service
TOEFL, PO Box 899, Princeton, NJ 08541, USA
Tel: 609 921 9000
Responsibility for the TOEFL programme is shared by the College Board, the Graduate Record Examinations Board and Educational Testing Service. Policy is determined by a Policy Council.

Status

Single-subject examination.

Aims

To provide valid test scores indicating the English proficiency of non-native speakers seeking admission to colleges and universities in the United States and Canada. Also used in other countries by institutions where English is the medium of instruction. Each institution using TOEFL scores establishes its own acceptable range of scores. These are often used to place students in courses of the appropriate level of difficulty, or for determining whether additional study of English is required before an applicant can study successfully in English.

Level

TOEFL is designed for (US) grade 11 students and above. See also **Results** on page 24.

Availability

Given only at centres established by the Educational Testing Service, which are in approximately 135 countries throughout the world. It is administered 12 times a year, once a month.

Content

The times and number of questions given below are approximations as there may be minor variations in any one test.
Time Approximately 3 hours, including time for admission procedures.
Since 1978 the test has been divided into 3 sections:

Section 1 Listening Comprehension (40 minutes – 50 items)

There are 3 parts, each involving listening to a tape recording in standard American English.

Part A Each item is a recorded statement which candidates have to match to one of 4 printed sentences, choosing the one most similar in meaning to the one heard on the recording.
Part B Candidates hear a number of short conversations, each followed by spoken questions; the candidate is required to choose an appropriate answer based on each conversation.
Part C Candidates hear a number of short talks, conversations or presentations; each is followed by several spoken questions. Candidates must choose one of the answers printed in the test book for each question heard on the recording.

Section 2 Structure and Written Expression (25 minutes – 40 items)

This section is divided into 2 parts:

Part A This is to test understanding of grammar and syntax. From 4 responses provided for each question, the candidate must choose the word or phrase that best completes a given sentence.
Part B This is to test a knowledge of the structure of written English. Candidates must identify the words or phrases in a given sentence that would not be accepted in standard written English.

Section 3 Reading Comprehension and Vocabulary (45 minutes – 60 items)

This is divided into 2 parts and is designed to test ability to understand academic reading material as well as the meaning and use of words and idiomatic phrases.
Part A In each item candidates must choose an appropriate substitute for a designated word or phrase in the context of a sentence.
Part B Candidates are given a number of short passages chosen to represent academically oriented subjects of an expository nature. Questions are based on each text.

Results

Results are given as a score report, which is sent to the candidate and institutions named by the candidate. Current TOEFL score reports show the score on each of the three sections of the test and the total score. The Educational Testing Service advises institutions to interpret the scores according to their needs. At some British universities a score of 550 is the required standard; candidates with a score of 450 and above can be accepted but would need further tuition in English.

An approximate comparison with the University of Cambridge Local Examinations Board examinations can be made:*

* *Note*: This comparison is based on observations in British universities and has not been provided or verified by the TOEFL programme.

TOEFL	University of Cambridge
685	Diploma in English Studies
550–500	Certificate of Proficiency
475–450	First Certificate in English

The TOEFL programme does not issue official score reports that are more than 2 years old.

Further information

There are several editions of the *TOEFL Bulletin of Information* (candidates in Europe should use the overseas edition for Europe) for use by applicants in registering for the test. A *Handbook for Examinees* (2 editions are available: United States/Canada and Overseas) and a booklet *Testing American Style* are sent to those who have registered. *Test and Score Manual, TOEFL Sample Test, Understanding TOEFL: Test Kit 1* and *TOEFL Research Reports* 1–15 are also available directly from the Educational Testing Service.

Copies of the *TOEFL Bulletin* are usually available through United States embassies and consulates or US Information Agency offices.

Candidates in Europe can register through:

CITO
National Institute for Educational Measurement
PO Box 1034, 6801 MG Arnheim, Netherlands

6 English Language Teaching Development Unit (ELTDU)

Title

6.1 Stages of attainment scale and test battery

Conducted by The English Language Teaching Development Unit Limited (ELTDU)
23 Market Square, Bicester OX6 7BR
Tel: Bicester (08692) 45255

Status A privately-developed Attainment Scale and Test Battery designed for commercial or industrial organizations. Results obtained from this test are not intended to be entrance qualifications for academic courses.

Aims To provide an overall scale by which stages of language ability throughout an organization can be defined and measured objectively.
To provide a scale which defines language levels not only in linguistic terms, but also in terms of what tasks employees at particular stages can be expected to perform with the language at their disposal.
To provide a battery of items as a means of testing individuals to determine their language level, and hence determine what tasks they are able to perform which require the use of English.

Levels The Test Battery does not assess candidates by pass/fail criteria. Instead, it assesses the language ability of all candidates and places them on a broad, 8-point Scale of Attainment. The scale ranges from Stage A (the employee has only just begun to learn English. He is still in the process of learning the basic structures of the language and in no way can be said to 'speak English') to Stage H (equivalent to an articulate, educated native speaker with a very full command of the language).

Availability The Scale and Test Battery are not available for sale to individuals. Organizations and institutions may purchase the reproduction rights to the Scale and/or Test Battery on application to ELTDU.

Content The Test Battery consists of a Pre-Selection Test and 3 Stage Tests. The format of each of the 3 Stage Tests is similar.

Pre-Selection Test

To determine an employee's approximate stage of attainment. The Test is divided into 8 stages, labelled A to H, corresponding to the 8 stages on the Attainment Scale. Each stage contains 20 questions. For convenience the Test is divided into 2 parts:

I – Stages A–F 1 hour
  Section 1: Listening and speaking
  Section 2: Reading and writing
II – Stages G and H 20 minutes
  Section 1: Listening and speaking
  Section 2: Reading and writing

Stage Tests

To give a more detailed assessment of an employee's language ability. One of the 3 Stage Tests is administered after the Pre-Selection Test to match an employee's language ability with a relevant stage on the Attainment Scale. Each Stage Test has 4 components: Reading, Writing, Listening and Speaking. The first 3 components take 90 minutes. The Speaking component, which consists of an interview in a simulated situation, takes 10–20 minutes.

Results

The results obtained from the Test Battery assign an employee to one of the 8 stages on the Attainment Scale. Each stage is described in 2 ways:

1 For administrators Information on language ability is stated in practical terms covering the various kinds of tasks which employees may have to carry out in English.

2 For teachers A specification of the linguistic requirements for carrying out the given tasks adequately, indicating what an employee at a particular stage on the Attainment Scale can and cannot be expected to do. This specification is intended to form the basis of future language training.

Further information

Available from ELTDU:
Stages of Attainment and Test Battery – general information; inspection copies.

7 English Speaking Board (International) Limited (ESB)

Title 7.1 Oral assessments in spoken English as an acquired language

Conducted by The English Speaking Board (International) Limited (ESB)
32 Roe Lane, Southport, Merseyside PR9 9EA
Tel: Southport (0704) 34587

Status Single-subject examinations held at 10 levels.

Aims To assess the ability to use spoken English of candidates for whom English is not the native language. The assessments are intended to stimulate and encourage lively and vital use of speech in communication. All candidates are assessed in relation to their cultural background and to the language they will use in the environment in which they will work and live.

Levels The assessments are made at 10 levels from the earliest stages of learning to complete fluency. The grades are suitable for candidates of all ages and all levels of achievement.

Foundation Stages 1–3 Designed for beginners of all ages.

Intermediate Stages 1–3 Designed for those who have made marked progress in using English.

Advanced Stages 1–3 Designed for those using English fluently and confidently at an advanced level in the course of everyday work.

Certificate in English as an Acquired Language Designed for candidates who will have to teach, lecture or conduct international business in English. Candidates should have reached bilingual competence in their fields.

Availability The Certificate in English as an Acquired Language is available only to mature candidates. All other assessments are available to candidates of all ages and are available throughout the United Kingdom and elsewhere by arrangement with the Secretary. Assessments can be arranged for short-term holiday course candidates in the United Kingdom.

Content The assessments are usually made in the presence of a small participating group who may ask questions and join in the discussion when appropriate.

Foundation Grades 1–3 (6–12 minutes per candidate)

a **Talk** Candidates give basic facts to their listeners about a subject in which they are interested.

b **Prepared reading** Candidates prepare a short passage of prose appropriate to their own level of attainment, lasting not more than 2 minutes.

c **Impromptu speaking** Candidates are expected to respond to simple questions from the group or the assessor. These may arise at any time during the assessment.

Intermediate Grades 1–3 (12–18 minutes per candidate)

a **Project** Candidates present a topic in which they are interested, with the use of relevant visual aids, and respond to questions from the assessor and the group.

b **Prepared reading** Candidates read aloud a prepared passage of prose or poetry of their own choice.

c **Meeting situations** Candidates are expected to respond appropriately to situations outlined by the assessor, such as explaining a course of action, or giving advice or directions.

d **Impromptu speaking** This may arise at any point of the assessment, either from earlier sections or from the candidate's own interests and experience.

Advanced Grades 1–3 (20–30 minutes per candidate)

a **Project** Candidates present a topic in which they are interested, supported by visual aids, and respond to questions from the assessor and the group. Candidates should demonstrate their ability to present their material to an informed but non-specialist audience.

b **Prepared reading** Candidates read a prepared passage from a book, an article in a quality newspaper, a journal, non-technical professional literature or from an anthology which they have enjoyed. They should place it in context and recommend it to their listeners. Passages containing dialogue are recommended but not essential.

c **Meeting situations** Candidates are expected to respond appropriately to situations outlined by the assessor. These may entail explanation or problem solving, and will require greater initiative and originality than are called for at the Intermediate Stages.

d **Comprehension** Candidates are expected to respond to questions on a passage of topical interest read to them by the assessor.

The passage is chosen to assess their ability to recognize implication and connotation, and to enable them to respond to deductive questions or to explore the subject matter in greater depth. Where appropriate, passages will be relevant to candidates' national and cultural backgrounds.

e **Impromptu speaking** This may arise at any time during the assessment and range over a variety of topics in the preceding sections, or other topics of interest to candidates. Candidates are expected to deal effectively with questions and opinions from the group, to conduct and control the discussion with style and authority, to initiate discussion and themselves pose relevant questions to stimulate audience participation.

Certificate in English as an Acquired Language
(Approximately 1 hour per candidate)

a **Vocational presentation** Candidates present a 10-minute lecture/demonstration related to their professional roles, supplemented by relevant visual aids. The presentation should be extempore, although notes consisting of no more than subject headings may be consulted.

b **Non-vocational presentation** Candidates prepare a 5-minute talk on some pursuit of artistic, humanitarian or sociological significance. The talk should be extempore, although notes consisting of no more than subject headings may be used. After the talk, candidates must lead a 2-minute discussion on their presentation with the group.

c **Reading** *i* Candidates prepare a passage of prose or poetry suitable for reading aloud. The text should be chosen from a journal (technical or non-technical), book or anthology which the candidate has read and appreciated. The extract must be introduced and placed in context so that the group can appreciate the significance of the piece.
ii The assessor selects a passage from a publication such as a quality newspaper for the candidate to read to the group.

d **Meeting a situation** Candidates are expected to respond appropriately to a situation outlined by the assessor. This may entail explanation, demonstration, persuasion, argument or advice, and will involve problem solving. A written or picture stimulus may be provided to present the situation.

e **Comprehension** Candidates are expected to respond appropriately to questions and opinions on a passage of topical interest read to them by the assessor.

f **Studies of the English-speaking world** Candidates are expected to choose and discuss some aspect of the history, customs or arts of the English-speaking world.

Results

Certificates and reports are awarded to all successful candidates. Certificates are awarded at 5 grades – Pass, Good pass, Very good pass, Credit and Distinction. Special weaknesses are pointed out to unsuccessful candidates and constructive advice given. Reports and certificates can be issued on the day of the examination.

Further information

Available from the English Speaking Board:
Guidelines and basic notes for teachers and examiners concerned with the syllabus of spoken English as an Acquired Language. General introductory notes for all organizers, teachers, tutors, parents and candidates. Lists of suitable books of prose and poetry.

8 General Medical Council (GMC)

Title

8.1 The PLAB Test

(The Professional and Linguistic Assessments Board's Test of Professional Knowledge and Competence and Proficiency in English)

Conducted by The General Medical Council
Professional and Linguistic Assessments Board
153 Cleveland Street, London W1P 6DE
Tel: London (01) 387 2556

Status This test is required by the General Medical Council for doctors requiring limited registration as medical practitioners in the UK. This registration is required before overseas-qualified doctors can begin their first appointment in the United Kingdom.

Aims To assess, separately, a candidate's proficiency in the English language and competence in medicine.

Level A professional level examination. The standard required is defined by the Board as that necessary to undertake safely employment at Senior House Officer level in a British hospital.

Availability All overseas-qualified doctors working to obtain limited registration are required to apply for entry to the test, although exemption may be granted in certain circumstances (individual enquiries about exemption should be addressed to the General Medical Council). Tests are normally held at least once a month, except in August. Tests are held at 6 centres: 3 in London, 2 in Edinburgh and one in Glasgow.

Content The full test consists of 2 components, one medical and one linguistic:

Language Component

a Comprehension of spoken English paper
b Written English paper
c part of the Oral examination

Medical Component

a Multiple Choice Question paper
b Medical Short Answer paper
c part of the Oral examination

Fuller details of the Language Component are given below:

Comprehension of spoken English Test (Practice test: $\frac{1}{4}$ hr; Actual test: $1\frac{1}{2}$ hrs)

1 The candidate hears 20 sentences and has to decide what function the speaker is trying to perform.

Example
'Show me where it hurts.'

a Seeking information *c* Making a statement
b Expressing surprise *d* Making a suggestion

2 The candidate hears 20 recorded sentences and must choose which of 4 adjectives best describes the attitude or mood conveyed by the speaker's intonation.

Example
'I'm just going to pop in a stitch or two.'

a Serious *c* Excited
b Authoritative *d* Reassuring

3 The candidate hears 20 recorded sentences and must choose the correct meaning given by the placing of stress.

Example
'*When* did you cut your hand?'

a Your hand and not your foot.
b What time did it happen?
c When did you cut it rather than bruise it?
d I know when your mother cut hers.

4 The candidate hears 20 recorded sentences and must choose the most suitable response.

Example
Patient 'I was in the kitchen getting lunch and I cut my finger.'
Doctor *a* You've bruised it, have you?
b Was this last night?
c Where were you at the time?
d With a knife, was it?

Written English Paper

There are 3 sections, which carry equal marks.

1 The candidate must write 300–500 words on one of 3 non-medical topics.

Examples

a Write an article for a popular magazine on the confidentiality of a doctor's dealings with his patients, indicating any possible circumstances in which its relaxation might be considered.
b Give some of the reasons why you decided to take up medicine as a profession.
c Write an article on preparation for retirement.

2 The candidate must write a passage about a particular situation either as an explanation to a non-medical person or as a letter to a non-medical person.

Examples
a You have as a patient an obese young woman whose complaint requires her to reduce weight drastically. Write down the actual words (200–300) you would use in advising her.
b A young niece has just started smoking cigarettes and you have been asked by her parents to write to her pointing out the dangers of this practice. Write a letter to her on this subject.

3 Cloze test. The candidate is asked to complete gaps in a piece of prose. Each gap requires a single word which is grammatical and makes sense in the particular context.

The Oral Examination (20 minutes)

The candidate is examined by two medical examiners. Its purpose is to assess the candidate's proficiency in spoken English and also his capacity to form sensible clinical judgments. One of the 2 examiners questions the candidate on clinical matters in the first 10 minutes, while the other listens and makes an assessment of the candidate's English. During the second 10 minutes the examiners change roles.

Results A pass is required before any overseas-qualified doctor may be granted registration by the General Medical Council. The General Medical Council notifies a candidate by letter to say whether he has passed or failed.

Further information Available from the Professional and Linguistic Assessments Board: *Advice to Candidates.*

9 Institute of Linguists Educational Trust

9.1 Examinations in English as a foreign language

Title

Conducted by

The Institute of Linguists Educational Trust
Mangold House, 24a Highbury Grove, London N5 2EA
Tel: London (01) 359 7445

Status

A unit/credit series of examinations set at 4 levels.

Aims

To provide a series of examinations assessing a candidate's communicative ability in performing authentic 'operations' or tasks in the English language. The examinations are designed for those learning English for occupational purposes.

Levels

The examinations are set at 4 levels up to and including the Institute's Grade II examination (approximately A level – see Appendix 1):

Level 1 Council of Europe Waystage level
Level 2 Council of Europe Threshold level +
Level 3 roughly equivalent to GCE A/O level
Level 4 roughly equivalent to GCE A level

Availability

At present the examinations are available only in draft form and therefore there may be restrictions on their availability. The final version of the examinations is expected to be available in 1985.

Available only to candidates whose mother tongue is not English. There are centres in Britain and a number of overseas countries.

Content

Level 1

Part 1 (11 minutes)

1 **Dialogue/Role play** After studying an application or official form, the candidate must respond to the examiner in an impersonal setting (eg respond to a policeman, a ticket collector, a customs official).
2 **Dialogue** To ask questions of the examiner in an impersonal setting (eg asking for direction, asking how to do something).

Part 2 (35 minutes)

1 **Aural comprehension** To transfer information from a spoken (recorded) text into tabular form. The monologue is heard twice and candidates are told the specific piece of information required before the text is heard.
2 **Recognition of written material** To recognize and demonstrate comprehension of common public notices (eg bus stop, left luggage).

Part 3 Cloze test (20 minutes)

Level 2

Part 1 (20 minutes)

1 **Responding to written material** To read short texts giving public information (eg holiday brochures, tourist guides, etc).
2 **Dialogue** To converse with the examiner in a friendly setting, asking and answering simple questions, expressing preferences, explaining circumstances, narrating events and justifying decisions.
3 **Aural comprehension** To listen for specific requests for information in a recorded text and to retrieve that information from a table. The text is a monologue which is heard once. The candidate has time to familiarize him/herself with the table before listening to the text.

Part 2 (45 minutes)

1 **Responding to a trilateral conversation** To listen to a recording of a trilateral conversation once only and answer a set of questions which can be read before the recording is heard.
2 **Composition** To write a letter of about 100 words on a given subject.
3 **Reading comprehension** To read simple instructions.

Part 3 Cloze test (20 minutes)

Level 3

Part 1 (Preparation – 30 minutes; Test – 25 minutes)

1 **Sustained speech** To speak from prepared notes giving an explanation of a process or organizational hierarchy which must demonstrate logical and sequential relationships.

2 **Dialogue** To discuss a course of action with one other and come to agreement.
3 **Dialogue** To argue a point of contention with one other from prepared notes. Candidates are given a position paper presenting arguments supporting both sides of a contentious issue and are given 20 minutes to prepare the arguments supporting the side they find more sympathetic.

Part 2 ($1\frac{1}{2}$ hours)

1 **Composition** To write a business letter to a colleague confirming the arrangements made in Part 1, Question 2. Candidates are given the necessary information and asked to include an agenda for the meeting.
2 **Report** To write a summary of about 200 words of the discussion in Part 1, Question 3.
3 **Listening comprehension** Candidates are given details of 3 characters involved in a conversation and the gist of the argument each is putting forward, before listening to the conversation. Selected words are omitted from the conversation and candidates have to produce an acceptable filler for each gap. The recording is played 3 times. The text is complete in the first playing.

Part 3 Cloze test (20 minutes)

Level 4

Part 1 (1 hour 40 minutes)

1 **Note taking** To take notes summarizing the main points of a 3-minute recorded monologue describing points for and against a course of action. The monologue is played twice.
2 **Listening comprehension** As for Part 2, Question 3 of the Level 3 examination but with less guidance. The recording is played twice.
3 **Reading and Writing** To read a text conveying a definite opinion, argument or point of view (eg a newspaper editorial) evaluating and commenting on the input.
4 **Writing** To write an informal piece of narrative, description or evaluation.

Part 2 (Preparation – 5 minutes; Test – 30 minutes)

1 **Notes** To inform the examiner of the contents of the notes taken

in Part 1 and deal with interruptions and requests for explanation.

2 **Cloze** The candidate is given a transcript of the listening comprehension test (Part 1, Question 2) and has to report to the examiner the gist of the conversation, conveying information about the attitudes, emotions, etc of the characters.

3 **Text** The candidate is given a copy of the reading and writing text (Part 1, Question 3) and has to report to the examiner the gist of the views expressed in it. The candidate also has to evaluate these views and justify his own response to them.

4 **Informal production** To convey to the examiner in speech the content of the candidate's answer to Part 1, Question 4.

Part 3 Cloze test (20 minutes)

Results Results will be graded Distinction, Pass or Fail. Any part of the examination in which a pass is not obtained may be retaken at a subsequent session.

Further information A draft syllabus is available from the Institute of Linguists Educational Trust.

Title

9.2 Certificates in English as a foreign language

Conducted by The Institute of Linguists Educational Trust
Mangold House, 24a Highbury Grove, London N5 2EA
Tel: London (01) 359 7445

Status A single-subject examination held at 3 levels.

Aims The Preliminary and Grade 1 Certificates are qualifications for students studying for non-academic and non-professional purposes, particularly students studying for pleasure. The Grade II Certificate is a practical qualification for occupational purposes.

Levels Examinations for Certificates are held at 3 levels. In addition, the Institute of Linguists holds Diploma examinations at two higher levels. See Appendix 1 for comparative levels of EFL examinations.

Preliminary Certificate An examination at which students may aim at the end of one year of part-time study.

Grade I Certificate A qualification roughly equivalent to GCE O level.

Grade II Certificate A qualification roughly equivalent to GCE A level.

Availability Available only to candidates whose mother tongue is not English. Candidates may enter for only one level of the examination at a time. Entries must be made through a registered Institute of Linguists centre. There are centres in Britain and a number of overseas countries. Examinations are held twice a year, usually in the last week in May and the first week in December.

Content

Preliminary Certificate (1 hour)

	Minutes	*Marks*
1 **Conversation** Conversing on one or more topics from a given list, with the examiner speaking at about 100–200 wpm.	5	11%
Examples of topics My friends and relatives; My travels; My district or town; Food and drink		
2 **Sustained speaking** Speaking on any point that has arisen in the conversation.	1	11%
3 **Situational conversation** Taking part in a conversation imagined as being in one of the places on a given list. The examiner offers a choice of 2 situations, asking the candidate to play one of the roles. The examiner takes the other role.	4	11%
Example In the restaurant. You are the head waiter. Take a customer's order for lunch. (The examiner will act as the customer.)		
4 **Aural comprehension** Answering in writing 10 open-ended questions on a passage of 100–200 words read aloud at about 100–120 wpm three times.	20	33%
5 **General knowledge of Britain** Candidates are asked to write short paragraphs on 10 topics from a list of 20.	30	33%
Examples The English Channel; Prince Charles; An anniversary; Bingo; Wimbledon; The Mersey.		

Grade I Certificate ($3\frac{1}{2}$ hours)

1 **Reading aloud** A passage of about 150 words to be read aloud at a speed of about 120 wpm.	2	6%
2 **Conversation** Conversing on one or more topics from a given list, with the examiner	7	6%

	speaking at about 100–120 wpm. Topics similar to those in Preliminary Certificate.		
3	**Sustained speaking** Speaking on any point that has arisen in the conversation.	2	6%
4	**Situational conversation** Taking part in a conversation imagined as taking place in one of the places on a given list. The examiner offers a choice of 2 situations, asking the candidate to play one role. The examiner takes the other role. *Example* In the street. A passer-by asks you where the police station is, and the best way to get there. (The examiner will act as the passer-by.)	4	6%
5	**Aural comprehension** Answering 10 questions on a passage of about 250 words read aloud twice at normal reading speed. Notes may be taken.	25	13%
6	**Dictation** Writing a passage of about 100 words dictated at a speed of about 100 wpm, excluding pauses. The passage is read 3 times.	20	13%
7	**Reading comprehension** A text of about 250 words with 10 free-response questions on it.	30	7½%
8	**Letter-writing** An informal letter of about 150 words dealing with personal matters. Choice of 3 subjects. *Example* A letter of thanks to a friend with whom you have been staying for a few days.	30	7½%
9	**Composition** A formal letter or short article of about 150 words on a subject of personal interest or common daily affairs. Choice of 3 subjects. *Example* A letter to a hotel enquiring about accommodation for yourself and family for a short holiday.	30	7½%
10	**General knowledge of Britain** Candidates are asked to write approximately 40 words on each of 5 topics from a list of 10 topics relating to aspects of life in Britain.	60	25%

Examples
London; British Rail; Secondary Education in England and Wales

Grade II Certificate (4 hours 20 minutes)

1	**Prepared talk** Speaking for 3 minutes on one of 6 topics of general interest given to the candidate 20 minutes before the examination. *Examples* Law and order; Daily newspapers; Building societies	3	6%
2	**Conversation** Conversing on topics arising from the prepared talk or on matters of general or personal interest.	8	6%
3	**Spoken summary** Summarizing briefly and answering questions on a text of 200 words. The candidate is allowed 5 minutes to study the text and may refer to it during the test.	9	13%
4	**Summary of speech** Writing a summary of about 100 words of a passage of about 300 words, read aloud twice at about 150 wpm. Notes may be taken during the readings.	30	25%
5	**Translation** Translating into the candidate's own language 2 passages each of 200–250 words.	90	25%
6	**General knowledge of Britain** Writing approximately 150 words on each of 3 topics. Topics are grouped in 3 sections – Geography, Institutions and Life. Topics must be chosen from at least 2 sections. *Examples* Geography – Yorkshire; Inland waterways; Shipbuilding; Institutions – banks; trades unions; The Prime Minister; Life – popular magazines; A General Election; Unemployment	120	25%

Results

A Pass must be obtained in all parts of the examination for the award of a Certificate. Any part of the examination in which a pass is not obtained may be retaken at any subsequent session.

Further information

Available from the Institute of Linguists:
Membership of the Institute of Linguists (booklet); syllabus of examinations; past examination papers; bibliography; *Introduction to the Examinations of the Institute of Linguists Educational Trust.*

Title

9.3 Diplomas in English as a foreign language

Conducted by The Institute of Linguists Educational Trust
Mangold House, 24a Highbury Grove, London N5 2EA
Tel: London (01) 359 7445

Status Single-subject examinations held at 2 levels. Passes satisfy the linguistic requirements for Membership and Associateship of the Institute of Linguists. Membership of the Institute is accepted as equivalent to a degree by the UK Department of Education and Science and Civil Service Commission.

Aims **Intermediate Diploma** To provide a language qualification for those following a course of study or employed in a post where English is an indispensable requirement for the work.

Final Diploma To provide a full professional qualification for translators and interpreters.

Levels Diploma examinations are held at 2 levels. In addition, the Institute of Linguists holds Certificate examinations at 3 lower levels. See Appendix 2 for comparative levels of ESP examinations.

Intermediate Diploma A post-A level qualification.

Final Diploma A qualification equivalent to a degree demanding a near-native command of the educated spoken and written language.

Availability Available only to candidates whose mother tongue is not English. Candidates may enter for only one level of the Diploma examinations at a time. Entries must be made through a registered Institute of Linguists centre. There are centres in Britain and a number of overseas countries. Examinations for the Intermediate Diploma are held twice a year, usually in the last week in May and the first week in December. Examinations for the Final Diploma are held only in May.

Content **Intermediate Diploma** (5 hours 55 minutes)

	Minutes	*Marks*
1 **Prepared talk** A prepared talk on a subject selected by the examiner from a list of 3 subjects brought by the candidate at the time of the examination.	4	7%
2 **Conversation** Conversing on matters arising from the prepared talk, or on matters of general interest, current affairs, cultural or social topics, and on more specialized subjects related to the candidate's work or study.	10	10%
3 **Spoken summary of a written text** Studying a text of about 250 words for three minutes and then giving a brief summary of it in two minutes. Reference may be made to the text	5	8%

while the summary is being made. The text is of a journalistic kind, dealing with a matter of common daily interest, eg motoring.		
4 **Spoken summary of a spoken text** Giving an oral summary of a passage of about 250 words read aloud once. Notes may be taken.	6	8%
5 **Summary** Writing a summary in 250–300 words of an article containing 600–800 words.	60	13%
6 **Translation** Translating a passage of 300 words from English into the candidate's mother tongue. The passage is on a semi-specialized topic such as general science, economics, political life, social problems, commerce, cultural life or public institutions.	60	10%
7 **Translation** Translating a passage of 250 words from the candidate's mother tongue into English. The passage is on a subject of general interest and is written in non-specialized language.	60	10%
8 **Background composition** Writing three compositions, each of about 250 words, on subjects dealing with the geography and economics, contemporary issues and institutions, 20th-century history and the arts of the English-speaking countries.	150	20%

Examples

The Scottish nationalists; Pubs and discos; Problems of government in India; Britain's influence in Africa

Final Diploma (10 hours 5 minutes – 12 hours 25 minutes)

1 **Prepared talk** A prepared talk on a subject selected by the examiner from a list of 5 subjects brought by the candidate at the time of the examination.	5	6%
2 **Aural comprehension** Short statements are read to the candidate. Questions are asked after each statement has been read. Notes may be taken during the reading.	8	6%

Example

James Herriot is a pseudonym for the world's most famous vet. The same wish for professional anonymity has made him place his stories in fictitious Darrowby, in the North Yorkshire dales. Yet fan mail addressed to this non-existent town reaches Herriot from all over the world.

Questions

1 Is James Herriot this man's real name?
2 Will you find Darrowby on the map of Yorkshire?

3 **Conversation** Discussion arising from the prepared talk and on other topics. 12 8%

4 Either **Essay** 750–1000 words on a current general topic. Choice of 3 subjects given. 180 20%

Examples
Writers in the English language in the 1970s; A famous British scientist.

Or **Précis** A summary in 600–750 words of an article, report or text of a speech on a current topic containing 1500–2000 words.

5 **Translation** Translating 4 passages, each of 250 words, 2 from English into the candidate's mother tongue and 2 from the candidate's mother tongue into English. The passages will deal with topics relating to current affairs, politics, social and cultural matters, and general economic and scientific subjects. 180 20%

6 **General knowledge of the English-speaking countries** Writing about 500 words on each of 3 questions dealing with the physical, technological, social, political and cultural aspects of the contemporary scene in the English-speaking countries. Choice of 9 subjects. 180 20%

Examples
Terrorists in Britain; The Kennedy family in US politics; The English novel in the 20th century

7 **Special subject** One of the following: 180 20%

a **Long essay** Candidates choose and submit for approval the titles of 6 unrelated topics within a field. One of the 6 topics is chosen by the Institute and the candidate informed at the beginning of this part of the examination. 1500 words to be written. Fields from which the topics must be chosen:

Geography and economics	Science and technology

The fine arts	Social life and institutions
A region of Britain	General or applied linguistics
English language teaching	Literature and thought in the 20th century
Business, industry and commerce	
Politics and recent history	

b	**Technical translation** 2 passages of about 500 words for translation into the candidate's mother tongue to test the candidate's specialized knowledge of a subject of his own choice. Dictionaries are allowed. Approved subjects (others may be considered upon application to the Institute 12 months before the exam):	180	20%

Aeronautical engineering	Agriculture	Economics
Chemical engineering	Chemistry	Law
Mechanical engineering	Physics	Textiles
Electrical engineering	Medicine	Transport
Marine engineering	Music	Politics

c **General interpreting**

i	translation at sight into the candidate's mother tongue	5	5%
ii	translation at sight into English	5	5%
iii	liaison interpreting, both ways	10	5%
iv	consecutive interpreting, both ways	20	5%

Results

A Pass must be obtained in all parts of the examination for the award of a Diploma. Any part of the examination in which a pass is not obtained may be retaken at any subsequent session.

Further information

As for **9.2.**

10 Joint Matriculation Board (JMB)

Title

10.1 Test in English (Overseas)

Conducted by The Joint Matriculation Board (JMB)
Manchester M15 6EU
Tel: Manchester (061) 273 2565

Status An entrance test in English, recognized by British universities and other institutions of higher education for admissions purposes.

Aim To test whether applicants to institutions of higher education have sufficient English to study on a British degree course.

Level At a level recognized as being approximately equivalent to Cambridge Proficiency. JMB will accept Grade C or better at GCE O level English Language as an acceptable alternative to the Test in English (Overseas). For comparative levels of EFL examinations, see Appendix 1.

Availability Intended for applicants seeking admission to courses in universities or other institutions of higher education. Candidates should not have English as their mother tongue, should have been educated abroad and should have lived in the UK for less than 5 years.

Available only through registered JMB examination centres. Examinations are held twice a year, in March and June.

Content The examination has 2 papers – written and aural – carrying equal marks.

Paper 1 Written English ($2\frac{1}{2}$ hours)

The Written English paper has 3 sections: Connected writing; Individual grammatical and vocabulary items; and Reading comprehension. The first 2 sections together carry 50%, and the Reading comprehension section also carries 50%

1 **Connected writing** Candidates are normally required to produce 2 or 3 pieces of connected writing. Each relates to a specific

situation, often illustrated with drawings or diagrams. Topics may include: instructions, general description, narrating a sequence of events, background to a sequence of events, outlining a process, setting out an argument.

Examples

1A Candidates are given a map of the town of Chilford.
- 1.1 Describe Chilford.
- 1.2 Write about the suitability of Chilford as a holiday town.

1B Candidates are given a diagram showing 3 types of bee.
- 1.3 Compare and contrast the 3 bees.

1C In forests old trees are cut down to allow new trees to grow. There are several systems used for clearing out the old crop and allowing the new one to grow. The diagram (given to the candidates) illustrates one such system of regeneration. In it, a–e show a section across the same piece of forest at 10 year intervals.
- 1.4 Use the diagram to help you outline the cycle of regeneration illustrated. Write about half a page.

2 **Individual grammatical and vocabulary items** A central range of frequent items tested in a modified cloze test.

Example

One word has been omitted from each line. Mark the place where you think a word is missing. In the space provided, write the word you think has been missed out.

Men always made masks. In early times animals provided a model. ____
Though most animal head shapes can made into masks fairly ____
easily, are few shapes which are difficult to make up as masks. ____

3 **Reading comprehension** Questions testing understanding of passages of a standard required to be read by the average first-year student at a British university. Passages are selected from any general semi-technical area studied at university. Most questions require candidates to understand the relationship between a written passage and a diagram to carry out a particular task which relates to the general purpose of the passage.

Example

The figure below [on page 48] summarizes 4 different ways of unloading meat from ship to rail waggon. On it the names refer to places the meat goes to. The arrows refer to the movement of meat from place to place. Choose the 3 methods which are referred to in the passage *Unloading Meat.* Tick the column where appropriate.

Example

	Method 1 Ship ▶ Quay ▶ Truck ▶ Shed ▶ Loading Bay ▶ Rail Waggon
	Method 2 Ship ▶ Truck ▶ Shed ▶ Loading Bay ▶ Rail Waggon
	Method 3 Ship ▶ Truck ▶ Loading Bay ▶ Rail Waggon
	Method 4 Ship ▶ Truck ▶ Rail Waggon

Paper 2 Aural (40 minutes)

Aural comprehension Candidates hear 2 spoken texts in the form of a discussion, dialogue, lecture, instructions, reading, etc, each of which may refer to a series of statements and diagrams. Candidates are then required to carry out a particular task which relates to the general purpose of the text.

Example
You will hear a talk about the drawings made by chimpanzees and children. You will hear the information twice. As you listen you should make notes so that later you can:

i identify the 9 sentences, from A–K below, which are about the development of a child. Number them in the order they occur. Write the numbers 1–9 in the boxes.

ii classify the diagrams (given to the candidate) by writing, above each diagram, an appropriate symbol from the key.

A shapes inside circles ☐
B single lines ☐
C human figures ☐
etc

Results

Candidates are required to satisfy the examiners in both the written and aural parts of the test.

Further information

Available from JMB:

Syllabus and regulations, Test in English (Overseas); past papers and tapes; examiners' reports; *Notes for the Guidance of Teachers.*

11 London Chamber of Commerce and Industry (LCCI)

Title

11.1 English for commerce

Conducted by The London Chamber of Commerce and Industry Examinations Board (LCCI)
Marlowe House, Station Road, Sidcup, Kent DA15 7BJ
Tel: London (01) 302 0261

Status Single-subject examinations also used as part of Group Certificates (see Appendix 3).

Aims The examinations are designed to test knowledge of written and oral English and the ability to use language efficiently and appropriately in a business context.

Levels **Elementary Stage** Designed to test basic knowledge of written English. Credit is given for the appropriate use of complex sentences, punctuation, vocabulary and grammatical accuracy.

Intermediate Stage Designed to test the ability to comprehend and use written English as a means of communication within a commercial or industrial context. Candidates whose mother tongue is not English are required to pass an oral test before they can be awarded a Certificate.

Higher Stage Designed to test knowledge of written English and the ability to use it efficiently and appropriately within a business context. Candidates whose mother tongue is not English are required to pass an oral test before they can be awarded a Certificate. For comparative levels of ESP examinations, see Appendix 2.

Availability All entries must be made through a recognized centre. Each year there are 4 testing sessions: Winter (March), Spring (May), Summer (June) and Autumn (November). The Higher Stage examination is not available at the Winter Series. Check in the timetable of examinations available from LCCI, or with local centres. (A list of centres is also available from LCCI.)

Elementary Stage (2 hours)

Marks

1 Composition 40

Candidates have to write approximately 200 words on one topic. A choice of 6 topics of a general commercial nature is given.

Example

a Plastics.

b The cultivation of a crop which is important for my country.

c It is sometimes said that bigger firms are better firms. Give your views on this statement, indicating whether you would prefer to work for a big firm or a small firm.

d Housing problems.

e Training for a career in a modern office

f Some different ways in which people get to their places of work.

2 Comprehension 30

A passage of about 300 words again on a topic of general commercial interest is given.

Example

Changes in shopping habits.

Some of the questions following the passage require short written answers derived from the context of the passage.

Example

Mention 3 ways in which a second car is used by housewives in the United States.

Other questions test specific vocabulary items.

Example

Explain very briefly what is meant by any 4 of the following words or phrases as they are used in the passage:

a matter of course; indispensable; estate agent; traditional; residential

3 Composition of a letter 30

Candidates are required to write a letter of about 100 words based on given information. The subject matter is not technical and requires the candidate to write as a private individual to an organization.

Example

Write a letter of not more than 100 words to the appropriate official in your town, urging that immediate steps be taken to remedy a serious defect in the town's drainage system. At present this is incapable of coping with the storm water during a heavy period of rain, so that low-lying streets are frequently flooded.

This is not only a source of inconvenience to the residents, but also a menace to public health. Include some specific details to substantiate your complaint.

Intermediate Stage (2 hours)

1 Composition 40

Candidates are required to write about 300 words on a topic connected with business or current affairs. A choice of 6 topics is given.

Example

a In what ways does branding of goods affect the consumer?

b In which of the 4 branches of trade – wholesale, retail, import, export – would you like to make your career?

c Discuss one of your country's natural assets which you think could be utilized more than it is at present to boost the country's economy.

d Discuss the problems faced by the small trader because of competition from larger units such as supermarkets.

e Suggest ways in which the educational system of your country could be improved.

f It has been said that today men are as fashion-conscious as women. Give your views on this statement.

2 Summary 30

Candidates are required to summarize an approximately 400 word passage in not more than 120 words, then supply a title. The passage is on a topic concerning current affairs or business.

Example

Organization of the office.

3 Composition of a letter 30

Candidates are asked to write a 150–200 word letter from given information. The candidate has to write in an official capacity to an organization about a straightforward business transaction.

Example

Write a letter on behalf of your company to be sent to all the company's customers, informing them that prices of paints sold by your firm will not be increased for the rest of this year despite rising costs. Point out that this is because of increased business and the fact that the majority of customers pay their accounts within a month of receiving their goods. Give details of the discounts which are designed to encourage the continuance of prompt payment. Lay out your letter correctly.

Higher Stage (3 hours) All the questions carry equal marks

1 **Composition**

A 400–500 word composition chosen from a number of topics requiring some knowledge of commercial practice and procedure. Candidates may be asked to give their answers in the form of a report.

Examples

In what ways does a public limited liability company obtain its capital?
How far does the state of the United States economy affect businessmen in the rest of the world?

2 **Comprehension**

Comprehension questions are given on a passage connected with current affairs or commerce.

3 **Summary**

Candidates are asked to summarize an approximately 500 word passage in not more than 180 words. Again the passage is on a commercial subject. Candidates may be asked to extract certain specific threads of narrative or argument from the passage.

4 **Composition of a letter**

Candidates are asked to write a letter from given information. The letter is from an organization to an individual concerning a specific transaction. This will involve a task such as an explanation of difficulties, requesting clarification, writing an apology, etc.

Oral test (Intermediate: 7–8 minutes; Higher: 8–10 minutes)

This is for candidates whose mother tongue is not English. The test is a face-to-face conversation between the candidate and the examiner.

Results

Candidates must apply for their results directly to their local centres. 50% is required for a Pass, 75% for a Pass with Distinction. Candidates who already possess a pass Certificate are eligible to sit again to obtain a Distinction or a prize.

Further information

Regulations, syllabuses and timetables, and past question papers are available from LCCI.

Students from Singapore, Malaysia, Sabah, Sarawak, Brunei and Hong Kong can obtain past papers, syllabuses, etc directly from: Federal Publications (S) Pte Ltd, Suite 420, Peace Centre, Sophia Road, Singapore 9, or Federal Publications (HK) Ltd, Evergreen Industrial Mansion, Wong Chuk Hong Road, Aberdeen, Hong Kong. In Cyprus, Greece, Malta and the Middle East, from: Bridgehouse Bookshop and Stationers, Bridgehouse Building, Byron and Grivas Digenis Avenue, PO Box 4527, Nicosia, Cyprus.

Title

11.2 Communication – use of English Secretarial Studies Certificate

Conducted by The London Chamber of Commerce and Industry Examinations Board (LCCI)
Marlowe House, Station Road, Sidcup, Kent DA15 7BJ
Tel: London (01) 309 0440

Status Examination in Group Certificate (see Appendix 3).

Aims To test candidates' ability to communicate through common written business documents. The aim is to encourage candidates to realize the importance placed by the business community on the quality of written communication.

Level Post O level standard (see Appendix 2).

Availability Entries must be made through recognized centres. The exam may be taken at any age. For details of the exam timetable, apply to LCCI.

Content *Time* 2 hours (Total marks – 100). There are usually 3 questions (sometimes 2). The use of a standard English dictionary is allowed.

1 Writing a business letter/memorandum

Candidates are asked to write business letters and/or memoranda from given information.

Example

The following advertisement appeared in a newspaper on 6 June 1979. Write a letter in reply to it.

Leaving college? Are you leaving college this summer and wondering what to do? If you have a good educational background with shorthand and typing qualifications, we may be able to help you. We have many different clients in Publishing, Banking, Advertising, Insurance, Property, Television, Films, Travel Agencies, etc with vacancies both at home and abroad. For an interview, write telling us about yourself, mentioning any holiday work which you have undertaken and the kind of career in which you would be interested.

Address your letter to Jane Johnson at Job Opportunities, 17 Short Street, London W1A 4EB.

2 Comprehension

A passage on a topic of a commercial or business nature is given. Candidates are asked to explain fully what is meant by certain expressions used in the passage. They are also asked to use the information in the passage to compose a business communication.

Example

Candidates are given a passage on flexitime and the task:

The adoption of flexible working hours is under consideration at the company where you are employed as secretary/assistant to the Personnel Officer, who is at present away from the office, but who has asked you to assemble any useful information on the benefits of variable working hours. Compose a memorandum outlining the advantages and disadvantages of this from both the employer's and the employees' point of view. (30 marks)

There is no passage set specifically for précis, but questions may ask for a summary of relevant parts of a passage or passages or comparison of 2 passages. (25 marks)

3 **Composition**

Candidates are asked to produce brief business communications from information provided. For example, candidates may be asked to draft a telex message, a telegram, a minute of a discussion, an advertisement, or a résumé of a telephone conversation.

Example

Read the following job description, then in approximately 35 words, compose an advertisement suitable for publication in a magazine or newspaper.

The Sales Director of a small toy manufacturing company (where flexible working hours are in operation) requires a Secretary/Personal Assistant. The successful applicant for this post will have had some years' experience in a responsible secretarial post and will have excellent shorthand and typing speeds. Some experience in selling would be desirable, but not essential since training will be given. This will be necessary since the secretary will be required to negotiate with clients in the Sales Director's absence. The applicant may also be required to accompany him on business trips both at home and abroad. There are 4 weeks' annual holiday, and the salary is negotiable.

Results

Candidates must pass all subjects in the same series to qualify for the Secretarial Studies Certificate. Candidates may be referred at the discretion of the Committee in not more than one section (see Appendix 3). The referred section must be taken and passed within one year of attempting the full examination.

A pass in Communication counts towards the Shorthand Typist Certificate, the Audio Typist Certificate, the Clerk Typist Certificate and the Word Processing Certificate.

A single-subject Certificate is awarded for each subject passed where the full Certificate is failed.

Results are sent to centres where candidates registered for the exam.

Further information

Regulations, syllabuses and timetables as well as past papers are available through LCCI.

Title

11.3 Communication – use of English Private Secretary's Certificate, Private and Executive Secretary's Diploma

Conducted by

The London Chamber of Commerce and Industry Examinations Board (LCCI)
Marlowe House, Station Road, Sidcup, Kent DA15 7BJ
Tel: London (01) 309 0440

Status Examinations in Group awards (see Appendix 3).

Aim The purpose of these examinations is to ensure that candidates' skill in English is appropriate for the needs of their work.

Level These are post A level examinations (see Appendix 2).

Availability All entries must be made through recognized centres. Normally candidates should be at least 20 years of age in the calendar year in which they take the Diploma, and 18 for the Certificate examination. For details of examination times, apply to LCCI or local centres.

Content *Time* $2\frac{1}{2}$ hours

Skills needed are the ability:

1 to write continuous English grammatically
2 to summarize
3 to compose letters, reports and other forms of business communication from given information
4 to use the style of English appropriate to the context
5 to understand what is read and be able to explain it

The paper usually consists of 3 questions but the number can vary. The use of a standard English dictionary is allowed.

1 Composition

This tests the candidates' ability to write a letter, report or other business document from data provided. Sufficient information needed for the answer is given, but candidates may have to add minor details and will be expected to show that they can select information relevant to the needs of the question.

Example

Your company has grown rapidly in recent years and this growth has caused problems of organization and communications. The Board of Directors has engaged a firm of management consultants to study the organization, propose any necessary changes, define the responsibilities of all executives and managers, and suggest improved means of communication. You are secretary to the managing director, who asks you to draft a memorandum to be sent to all staff announcing the decision. He is particularly anxious that all staff should understand what is about to be done, so that unnecessary fears will not arise.

2 Summary

Candidates may be asked to summarize facts, opinions, arguments and/or counter arguments in the passage given, or in part of it. Examiners will be marking on the degree to which all relevant facts are included, their logical arrangement, conciseness, clarity, and the use of language appropriate to the context.

3 Comprehension

Candidates are required to answer questions on a given passage. Questions may be set on the meaning of words, phrases or sentences in the passage. Candidates will be tested on their ability to interpret and act upon the facts given, on their powers of inference or reasoning, on their ability to discern the intention of the writer, or on the line of argument used.

Results

Candidates may be referred in one section of all the examinations, but must pass in the referred section within one year of attempting the full examination. The Communication – Use of English examination counts towards a Shorthand Typist Certificate, an Audio Typist Certificate and a Shorthand Typist Diploma or Audio Typist Diploma. Communication also counts towards the Information Processing Group Certificate, at Private Secretary's Certificate level (see Appendix 3). Candidates are notified of their results by the centre through which they registered for the examination.

Further information

See **11.2**

Title

11.4 Spoken English for industry and commerce (SEFIC)

Conducted by

The London Chamber of Commerce and Industry Examinations Board (LCCI)
Marlowe House, Station Road, Sidcup, Kent DA15 7BJ
Tel: London (01) 302 0261

Status

Single-subject examination run by the Commercial Education Scheme of the LCCI.

Aim

To test the ability of candidates whose mother tongue is not English to communicate orally in practical situations. The examinations are designed for non-native speakers who, in the course of business or for social purposes, have contact with English speakers in contexts where the ability to communicate orally/aurally is important.

Levels

Preliminary This requires the candidate to cope without too much difficulty in everyday situations in which the foreigner might find himself. A basic vocabulary of approximately 500 words is needed.

Intermediate This requires a good enough command of English to be able to communicate easily with acquaintances, colleagues or business contacts. A knowledge of vocabulary particular to the candidate's own business is needed.

Advanced This requires a very high standard of oral English. A candidate must be able to cope easily with any social or business situation in which he finds himself. Again, a knowledge of the specialized vocabulary of his own business is needed. Candidates need to demonstrate their ability to converse freely on topics of general interest and to be able to discuss in depth a subject of their own choice. At each level the examiner is looking for the candidate's ability *to*

communicate and takes account of mistakes of grammar and punctuation only when they impede understanding. The approach is entirely practical and non-academic. The examiner is not given word or structure lists which he must test, nor subject areas within which he must restrict his questioning.
See also Appendix 2.

Availability These examinations are for candidates whose mother tongue is not English and are available in the UK, the German Federal Republic, France and Switzerland. Candidates may enter at any time of the year, but entries must be submitted one month in advance.

Content The examination consists of face-to-face conversation and discussion between candidate and examiner.

Preliminary (20 minutes)

Section A

a General conversation on the candidate's personal history, work and interests.

b Development of 1 or 2 aspects of the general conversation.

Section B The candidate is asked to respond to spoken instructions given by the examiner relating to everyday objects which the examiner brings in.

Example
Pick up the handkerchief and give it to me.

Section C The candidate is asked to describe 2 pictures or photographs, 1 provided by the candidate and 1 provided by the examiner.

Section D The candidate is asked to play a part in an everyday situation described by the examiner, eg booking in at an hotel, asking the way, ordering a meal, buying a ticket, etc.

Intermediate (30–35 minutes)

Section A As for Preliminary.

Section B The candidate will be asked to take part in a role-playing or discussion exercise, which the examiner describes. It will be of a simple business or social nature, such as making enquiries, changing travel arrangements, complaining. Whereas at Preliminary level the candidate plays the role of a member of the general public, at Intermediate level he may be asked to be an official of some kind.

Section C The candidate will be asked to listen once to a recorded conversation. He will then be asked to give the main points of the conversation and will also be asked questions on it by the examiner.

Section D The candidate is given a letter and is given approximately half a minute to look through it. After he has done this he will be asked to explain some of the expressions in the letter.

Advanced (45–50 minutes)

Section A As for Preliminary.
Section B The candidate will be asked to describe or demonstrate some aspect of his work, or of his special subject and discuss it with the examiner. The details of the candidate's special subject must be submitted at the time the candidate enters for the examination. The candidate may bring material with him to illustrate his subject, eg samples, photographs, technical literature, catalogues, etc. The candidate will first be asked to talk for up to 5 minutes without interruption. The examiner will then question the candidate.
Section C The candidate is asked to listen once to a recorded conversation. He then has to explain briefly what the conversation was about and will also be asked questions on it by the examiner.
Section D The examiner will ask the candidate to choose 2 passages out of those offered. He will then be asked to study one of these passages and give a summary of it. If time allows, or if the first passage did not give enough evidence to the examiner of the candidate's ability to summarize, the candidate may be asked to summarize the second passage.

Results

Candidates are sent results slips showing the standard they reached expressed on a 4 point scale of Good/Satisfactory/Below Standard/Weak. The Pass standard is for Good and Satisfactory; Below Standard and Weak indicate a Fail. Certificates for successful candidates are normally sent within one month after the examination.

Further information

Syllabuses, *Teacher's Guide*, examination texts and tapes are available from LCCI.

12 North Western Boards

12.1 English as a second language

Title

Conducted by
a North West Regional Examinations Board
Orbit House, Albert Street, Eccles, Manchester M30 0WL
Tel: Manchester (061) 788 9521
b North Western Regional Advisory Council for Further Education
Town Hall, Walkden Road, Worsley, Manchester M28 4QE
Tel: Manchester (061) 702 8700

Status This examination is available in 2 versions:

a A Certificate of Secondary Education examination for students in British secondary schools.
b A joint North Western Regional Advisory Council/Union of Lancashire and Cheshire Institutes Certificate examination for full- or part-time students in British colleges of Further Education.

Aims The specific aims are to test the competence of ESL students in understanding and production within 5 broad language functions in spoken and written expository English: these are instruction, description, narration, narrative padding and process (see *Glossary*).

Level
a The level aimed at is that of the average 16-year old native speaker in Britain (see also **Results**).
b An elementary examination intended to provide a first formal assessment for the guidance of employers and for progression to further education.

Availability
a Available to non-native speakers in British secondary schools. No candidate can offer both English and English as a Second Language in the same year.
b Available to non-native speakers in British colleges of further education in the north-west of England and in some areas outside Lancashire and Cheshire. Not available overseas.

Content The examinations consist of 4 papers:

Paper 1 Continuous writing (1¾ hours + 15 minutes reading time) *Marks* 25%

There are 3 sections:

A Candidates are required to produce continuous expository writing in response to non-verbal information, eg graphs, tables, diagrams, etc.

Example
Candidates are given a map of a zoo with a key and the following:

Your friend wishes to visit the zoo on his way be car from Dorton to Paxton. He does not have a copy of the plan of the zoo. He wants to see the elephants, the chimpanzees, gibbons, baboons and spider monkeys, the vultures and the falcons, the pumas, lions, tigers and leopards, and the sea lions. He wants to have lunch. He wants to go for a walk in the garden.
Plan his tour of the zoo for him. Write clear instructions for him to follow.

B Candidates are required to show understanding of continuous prose.

Example
Given a passage on the process of bread making, candidates must order given sentences which outline the steps in bread making but which are in the wrong order.

C Candidates are required to use appropriate grammatical forms in context to complete a modified cloze test.

Example
The Saxons chose village sites there was good earth for farming ________
and water for man animals. First a cluster of wooden ________
houses went up. For protection this surrounded by a bank ________
etc.

Paper 2 Reading with understanding (1¾ hours + 15 minutes for reading the questions) *Marks* 25%

The paper has 3 sections:

A Candidates are required to respond in writing to show understanding of information presented in a variety of ways (maps, drawings, pictures, tables, texts, etc).

Example
Given a flow chart showing how rubber is manufactured, candidates must write a series of paragraphs describing how liquid rubber is made into a raincoat and a rubber mattress.

B Candidates are required to show understanding of continuous prose.

Example
Candidates read a passage entitled *The Ocean* and are then required to label diagrams illustrating features described in the text.

C Candidates are required to show understanding of the meanings and functions of words or definitions in specific verbal, pictorial or diagrammatic contexts.

Example
Candidates are given a series of definitions for 10 parts of a saddle. These definitions must be used to label a diagram of a saddle correctly.

Paper 3 Listening with understanding (Approximately 1 hour) — 25%

There are 2 parts. In each part candidates are required to show understanding of the meanings and functions of words or definitions in specific verbal, pictorial or diagrammatic contexts.

Example
Candidates hear a short lecture on a simple experiment. During the lecture notes can be taken. After the lecture has been given twice, candidates use their notes to label a series of diagrams describing the apparatus and the experiment.

Paper 4 Spoken English (10 minutes for preparation and then 5 minutes for speaking the 2 parts of the test) — 25%

Candidates are required to give a spoken response appropriate to the context of a set task. The responses are recorded and assessed by the class teacher. The recordings and assessment marks are then sent to the Boards for moderation.

Example
Candidates are given pictures showing three different types of soldier. Candidates are asked to make notes during the preparation period, but these cannot be used when the candidate is speaking. The task is to compare the 3 soldiers in a talk of not more than 5 minutes to the assessor.

Results

a Results are expressed in the form of Grades 1 to 5. A 16-year-old pupil of average ability and application may reasonably expect to secure Grade 4. A 16-year-old pupil whose ability is such that he might reasonably have attained Grade A, B or C at GCE O level may expect to secure Grade 1. The result of a pupil whose performance is inferior to Grade 5 is shown as Ungraded.

b Results slips are sent to the colleges, each candidate's results being in the form of a single percentage mark showing overall performance. Passes are awarded at 3 grades: 40-49% Pass; 50–69% Credit; 70–100% Distinction.

Further information

a Available from the North West Regional Examinations Board: Syllabus for the English as a Second Language Examination, and *English as a Second Language – Notes for the Guidance of Teachers.* A specimen tape and commentary for the assessment of the spoken English paper are available on loan.

b Available from the North Western Regional Advisory Council: *The Examination Scheme and Syllabus (Booklet 04). Notes for the Guidance of Teachers*. Specimen tapes and notes on the assessment of the spoken English paper are available to participating colleges.

13 Oxford Delegacy of Local Examinations (Oxford)

Title
13.1 University of Oxford Delegacy's Examinations in English as a Foreign Language

Conducted by Oxford Delegacy of Local Examinations (Oxford)
Ewert Place, Summertown, Oxford OX2 7BZ
Tel: Oxford (0865) 54291

Status Examinations at 2 levels in the comprehension and production of written English. Planned in conjunction with the ARELS Committee and intended to complement the ARELS oral test (see 2.1).

Aims To test performance in practical reading and writing those tasks candidates might be expected to experience while in Britain. (As the Delegacy's overseas centres increase, it is planned to introduce gradually content which is more culturally specific to the examinations.) The examinations are designed primarily for non-literary students who are studying or wish to study in Britain.

Levels **Preliminary level Certificate** A lower intermediate examination considered below the level of the Cambridge First Certificate of English. The emphasis at this level is on whether a candidate has sufficient reading and writing skills to 'survive' in English. The examination is designed to complement ARELS Preliminary Certificate (see Appendix 1).

Higher level Certificate An intermediate examination considered as slightly below Cambridge Proficiency in English. At this level candidates are expected to handle functional writing with ease and should be able to understand and reproduce changes in register. This examination is designed to complement ARELS Higher Certificate (see Appendix 1).

Availability At present the Preliminary level Certificate examination is administered in March and November and the Higher level in May. Ultimately the Higher level Certificate examination will be offered twice a year.

Applications are accepted for those candidates entered through accredited centres.

There are 2 papers. Candidates are permitted to use an English–English dictionary in both.

Paper 1 Writing (2 hours)

Among the items tested are: writing formal/informal letters; initiating and responding to letters; ability to write connected prose on topics relevant to any candidate's situation in the form of messages, notices, signs or telegrams. Candidates are given the number of words they should write for each question. There are 7 questions.

Question 1 is a situational composition of about 150 words from a choice of 4 topics. Questions give notes, drawings, advertisements, etc to elicit the answer.

Example
Write a report for other employees in your company who are coming to England. The idea is to tell them what to expect and how to enjoy themselves in England. Here are some notes that might help:

Weather, rain, umbrellas; Banks, money; English families; Pubs, beer, games

Question 2 requires the candidate to write a letter of about 150 words from a choice of 3 situations.

Example
You sent your camera film away to be developed and enclosed a cheque for the full amount. Your photographs have just arrived with a bill. Write a letter to the company pointing out their mistake. Your letter must be correctly set out.

Question 3 gives candidates a dialogue which they have to convert to a message.

Example
Write the message (about 40 words) you would leave for Mrs Murphy after the following conversation. (Imagine you are Ray.)

Mrs Naylor	Hello. Is Mrs Murphy in?
Ray	Hello Mrs Naylor. I'm afraid she's out at the moment. She's gone shopping and she said she'd be a couple of hours.
Mrs Naylor	Oh dear! Perhaps you can help. My hairdryer has broken and when I phoned Mrs Murphy earlier she said I could borrow hers.
Ray	I'll get it for you then. (He fetches the dryer.)
Mrs Naylor	Thanks! I'll bring it back about 6. If she needs it before then, ask her to give me a ring or come over.
Ray	All right. I'm going out soon, so I'll leave her a message. Goodbye.

Questions 4 to **7** are practical exercises requiring the candidate to write for given specific situations.

Examples
Blue sparks and a burning smell came from the electric kettle last time you used it. Write a note warning others not to use it. (About 3–5 words.) You have bought a birthday card for your teacher. What greeting do you write inside? (About 5 words.)

Paper 2 Reading comprehension (2 hrs 10 mins, including 10 minutes' reading time)

The level expected in receptive skills is higher than that expected in the productive skills tested in Paper 1. This tests candidates' ability to use a dictionary, to fill in forms, to follow instructions, to read for the general meaning of a text and to select specific information from a text.

Examples
In one question candidates must complete a patient questionnaire based on personal information. In another, candidates are given an extract from a dictionary which they must use to decide if given sentences are correct. They are required to rewrite incorrect ones.

The London train pulled in on time.

.... ☐

He pulled out his stomach to make himself less fat.

.... ☐

Other questions require candidates to match written descriptions or instructions with a corresponding drawing/map.

Higher level Certificate

There are 2 papers to be worked on the same day. As with the Preliminary level, the same broad pattern of testing production skills in Paper 1 and receptive skills in Paper 2 is followed. The level expected of receptive skills is higher than that of productive skills. An English-English dictionary may be used in both papers; questions in Paper 2 require the use of a dictionary.

Paper 1 Writing (3 hours)

Among the items tested are: realistic writing tasks, eg a report, a curriculum vitae, etc, of about 400 words; letters (usually three) to test ability to handle register; summary and/or expansion exercises; and functional writing as in the Preliminary level but more sophistication in handling the tasks is required.

Example
In one question the candidate is required to write 2 letters based on the same situation, each requiring a different register:

You have been to stay with a friend and his or her family and you wish to thank them. Write 2 letters, one to the friend, whom you know well, and one to an older member of the family with whom you are slightly acquainted.

Paper 2 Reading comprehension (3 hours)

Among the items tested are: a form to fill in, based on complex information; comparison and correction of 2 sources of the same information; sorting mixed-up information; using a dictionary to correct spelling mistakes, rewrite sentences and complete incomplete sentences; skimming text to answer comprehension questions; and rewriting material to show comprehension.

Example
In one question candidates are asked to write to a newspaper pointing out factual mistakes in an article about an assault case. The candidate is required to take the role of the person assaulted and has the newspaper article and an official report on the case on which to base an answer.

Results

Results are issued through the centres. At present there are 3 pass levels: Distinction, Credit, and Pass. There are 2 grades of failure: Fail 1 and Fail 2.

Further information

Copies of past question papers, reports and details of fees are available from the Oxford Delegacy of Local Examinations.

14 Pitman Examinations Institute (PEI)

Title **14.1 English**

Conducted by Pitman Examinations Institute (PEI)
Godalming, Surrey GU7 1UU
Tel: Godalming (04868) 5311

Status A single-subject examination set at 3 levels.

A pass at Elementary level satisfies the English language requirement of PEI's Basic Secretarial Group Certificate and Basic Commercial Group Certificate.

A pass at Intermediate satisfies the English language requirement of the Secretarial and Commercial Group Certificates.

A pass at Advanced satisfies the English language requirement of the Higher Commercial and Higher Secretarial Group Certificates. See Appendix 3 for Group Certificate requirements.

Aims To assess a candidate's ability to write clear, grammatically correct English without the aid of reference books, and to read contemporary English with understanding.

These examinations are intended for candidates whose mother tongue is English, but may be entered by overseas candidates. It is recommended that candidates who have reached the standard of English language (NCE) Advanced (see **14.2**) should be able to attempt the Intermediate examination.

Levels **Elementary** Set at a level approximately equivalent to a high CSE/low GCE O level pass.

Intermediate Set at a level approximately equivalent to a high GCE O level pass.

Advanced Set at a level higher than GCE O level but lower than GCE A level.

Availability Available only through educational establishments registered as PEI examination centres (over 4000 worldwide). Examinations can be held at any time of the year at dates arranged by centres.

Content The format of the papers at the 3 levels is broadly similar.
(*Time* Elementary – 2 hours; Intermediate – $2\frac{1}{2}$ hours; Advanced – 3 hours)

1 Listening comprehension A passage of contemporary prose is read aloud twice at normal reading speed. Candidates write answers in complete sentences to 5–6 free-response questions based on the passage or reproduce in continuous prose the main points made in the passage. During the 1-minute interval between readings the candidate may make notes. *Marks*

		Marks
Elementary	Passage of approximately 300 words	20
Intermediate	Passage of approximately 400 words	20
Advanced	Passage of approximately 500 words	20

2 Personal writing A choice of topics or situations is given.

Elementary

A composition or letter of approximately 250 words from a choice of 3 factual, descriptive or narrative subjects. One subject is a detailed situation. 40

Examples

a Which animal would you choose as a pet, and why?

b While you are waiting for a train, you put down your suitcase and go to buy a magazine. As you return, you see a man pick up your suitcase and walk away with it. You chase after the man and catch him up, but he insists the suitcase is his. A policeman comes to see what the noise is about and makes the man open the case. The first thing he sees in the case is your passport. The policeman takes the man away. You dash back to the platform, but you have missed your train. Describe the whole episode from the time you went to buy the magazine until you return to find that your train has gone. You may invent any detail you like to make the story interesting.

Intermediate 40

A composition or letter of approximately 350 words usually from a choice of 2 situations dealing with subjects expected to be within the candidate's experience.

Example

Schooldays are said to be the happiest days of one's life. Describe the happiest term you ever spent at school showing what made it happy.

Advanced 40

Approximately 500 words from a choice of 2 topics, one of which gives some suggested points in note form.

Examples

a To what extent should subjects taught in schools and colleges be decided by the students?

b Using some or all of the following points together with any ideas of your own you might have, discuss the following statement: 'Sport should be played for enjoyment rather than for profit or national prestige'.

Even bad players enjoy sport – good players deserve to be paid for their efforts – great sportsmen bring fame to their countries – professional sport encourages cheating and violence – sport brings in money for the community – sport is like all entertainment and should be paid for.

3 **Reading comprehension** A passage of contemporary prose, with questions based on the passage testing understanding of the main ideas and the language employed.

Elementary 20

A passage of approximately 300 words with 10 questions either multiple choice or free-response.

Intermediate 20

A passage of approximately 400 words with 10 questions either multiple choice or free-response.

Advanced 40

A passage of approximately 500 words with 8–12 free-response questions to be answered in the candidate's own words to show an understanding of the author's ideas and techniques.

4 **Grammar**

Elementary 20

Ten multiple choice questions requiring candidates to choose the grammatically correct sentence, the appropriate vocabulary for a given situation, the meaning of an idiomatic expression, or the correct rewritten version of a sentence.

Example

When Tom 'let the cat out of the bag', he

a enabled it to escape
b copied someone else's answer
c gave away a secret
d had just one idea in his head

Intermediate 10

Five sentences, each containing at least one error of spelling, syntax, idiom or usage. Sentences to be rewritten correctly.

Example

That boy's brother had a fatal accident as a result of which he died.

Advanced

There are no grammar questions at the Advanced level.

5 **Punctuation**

Intermediate only 10

An unpunctuated passage or conversation of approximately 50 words to be punctuated.

There are no punctuation exercises at Elementary or Advanced levels.

Results

Scripts are marked Pass (60%+) or Fail. First Class Pass (75%+) is awarded at Intermediate and Advanced levels only. Weakness slips indicating areas of inadequate performance are issued to candidates who fail an examination.

Further information

Available from PEI:
Regulations and syllabuses; *List of Most Commonly Misspelled Words*; specimen examination papers; examiners' reports for recent years.

Title

14.2 English as a Foreign Language and English Language (NCE)

Conducted by

Pitman Examinations Institute (PEI)
Godalming, Surrey GU7 1UU
Tel: Godalming (04868) 5311

Status

Single-subject examinations.

A pass at Intermediate (English Language (NCE)) or Higher Intermediate (English as a Foreign Language) satisfies the English language requirement for PEI's Basic Secretarial and Basic Commercial Group Certificates. A pass at Higher Intermediate (English Language (NCE)) or Advanced (English as a Foreign Language) satisfies the English language requirement for the Secretarial and Commercial Group Certificates. An Advanced (First Class) Pass (English Language (NCE)) is a qualifying subject for the Higher Secretarial and Commercial Group Certificates. See Appendix 3 for Group Certificate requirements.

Aims

EFL examinations designed to test a candidate's grasp of general English. For candidates in overseas countries where English Language is the common medium of communication in business and commerce, English Language (NCE) is more appropriate.

English as a Foreign Language is offered as 2 syllabuses: Syllabus L is appropriate for those candidates studying 'English' as a foreign language and Syllabus C is for those candidates who wish to use English for personal, travel, work or educational purposes. Syllabus C examination tests communicative skills rather than the correct usage of grammatical structure.

Levels

Each subject is offered at 4 grades: Elementary, Intermediate, Higher Intermediate, Advanced.

The Elementary and Intermediate stages are lower level examinations set at a level below that of Cambridge First Certificate. The Advanced stages are at a level between Cambridge First Certificate and Cambridge Proficiency. See Appendix 1 for comparative levels.

Availability Available only through educational establishments registered as PEI examination centres (over 4000 worldwide). Examinations can be held at any time of the year at dates arranged by centres.

Content

English as a Foreign Language (Syllabus L) (Elementary) (2 hours)

		Marks
1	**Dictation** 5 simple sentences read aloud at normal speed twice, and once more slowly with punctuation given.	20
2	**Aural comprehension** 5 questions are read aloud twice; candidates must give short answers in complete sentences.	20
3	**Essay** About 120 words of a descriptive nature based on personal knowledge; choice of 3 titles.	40
4	**Grammar** 20 multiple choice questions where the candidate must select the correct word(s), structure(s), etc to complete a sentence.	20

English as a Foreign Language (Syllabus L) (Intermediate) ($2\frac{1}{2}$ hours) and English Language (NCE) (Elementary) ($2\frac{1}{2}$ hours)

1	**Dictation** A connected passage of approximately 100 words is read aloud at normal speed twice, and once more slowly with punctuation given.	20
2	**Aural comprehension** A 150 word passage is read aloud twice; candidates must write short answers to printed questions based on the passage.	20
3	**Essay** 180–200 words of a descriptive or narrative nature; choice of 3 titles.	40
4	**Grammar** 20 multiple choice questions where the candidate must select the correct word(s), structure(s), etc to complete a sentence.	20

English as a Foreign Language (Syllabus L) (Higher Intermediate) and English Language (NCE) (Intermediate) ($2\frac{1}{2}$ hours)

1	**Dictation** A connected passage of approximately 130 words is read aloud at normal speed twice, and once more slowly with punctuation given.	20

2 **Aural comprehension** A 180-word passage is read aloud twice; candidates must reproduce in writing the central points of the passage. Notes may be made during the one-minute interval between readings.

3 **Essay** About 240 words of a descriptive or narrative nature, a discussion, or a letter; choice of 4 titles. 40

4 **Grammar** 20 multiple choice questions where the candidate must select the correct word(s), structure(s), etc to complete a sentence. 20

English as a Foreign Language (Syllabus L) (Advanced) and **English Language (NCE) (Higher Intermediate)** (3 hours)

1 **Dictation** A connected passage of approximately 160 words is read aloud at normal speed twice, and once more slowly with punctuation given. 10

2 **Aural comprehension** A 210-word passage is read aloud twice; candidates must reproduce in writing the central points of the passage. During the 1-minute interval between readings, the candidate may take notes. 20

3 **Essay or letter**

a Presentation of an argument or outline of a problem; approximately 300 words; choice of 3 titles. 30

b Writing a 100-word conversation on a given topic in either direct or reported speech. 20

4 **Written comprehension** Objective questions testing understanding of the ideas, idioms and vocabulary in a passage of approximately 100 words. 9

5 **Grammar** 11 multiple choice questions where the candidate must select the correct word(s), structure(s), etc to complete a sentence. 11

English Language (NCE) (Advanced) (3 hours)

1 **Aural comprehension** A 240-word passage is read aloud twice; candidates must reproduce in writing the central points of the passage. 15

2 **Composition**

a Presentation of an argument or outline of a problem; approximately 400 words; choice of 3 titles. 35

b Writing a letter for a given situation showing the ability 20 to select the right words and tone to fit a particular situation; no choice of topic.

3 **Written comprehension** Objective questions testing understanding of the ideas, idioms and vocabulary in a passage of approximately 350 words. 30

English as a Foreign Language (Syllabus C)

The syllabus is defined in terms of 7 'Domains of Language Use'. Any one paper includes tasks related to three domains. The domains are:

1 Domestic life
2 Buying and selling
3 Public and official services and information
4 Travel
5 Work
6 Entertainment
7 Education

Language activity related to these domains is further specified in terms of:

Locations; Social interactions; Topic areas; Text types.

For example, within the domain of *travel* a task might involve the topic of *holidays*, by requiring the candidate to write a *letter* (Text type) to a firm that rents holiday cottages/villas (Social interaction) reserving a particular cottage or villa that the candidate chooses from information listed in a brochure to match specified requirements.

The levels tested are the same as for Syllabus L and the distinction between levels is made in terms of the complexity of the responses each requires. Assessment is based upon 'adequate' performance on the tasks, a standard of 7 adequate answers out of 12 being the minimum acceptable; these must include one from each of the main reading, writing and listening questions.

Each paper is divided into 2 parts:

1 **Reading and writing** All questions are compulsory. Candidates are given authentic texts, eg newspaper articles, advertisements, letters, etc and are required to show understanding by extracting and transferring relevant information from the texts to complete forms, lists, flow charts, graphs, and to write letters, notes, messages, advertisements, etc.

Examples (Advanced)
Candidates are required to read an article from *The Guardian* called 'The

dream that never became a job' about graduates, particularly women graduates, finding employment. Candidates are asked: Explain the title to someone who asks you what it means.

Plot the graph below showing the percentage of graduates who could not find a job 6 months after leaving university.

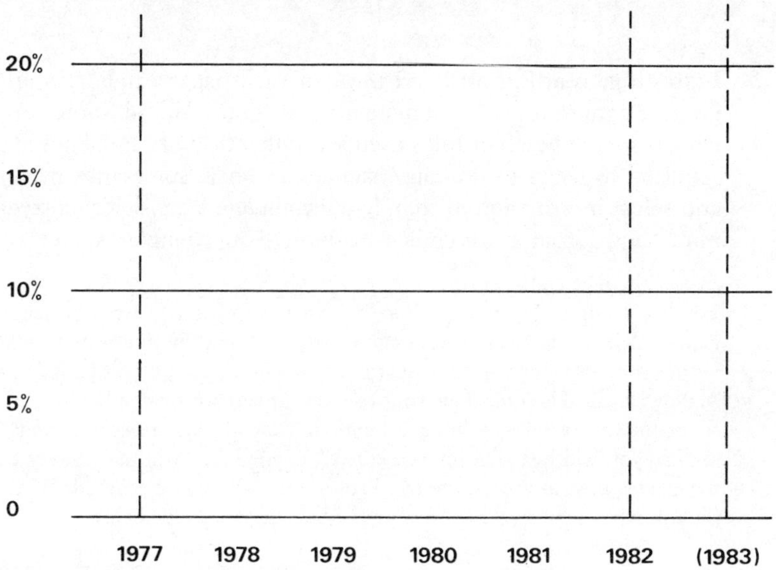

Mark on the 1982 line:

△ to indicate % of men

□ to indicate % of women

You are going to give a talk to a group of women graduates. Make some notes in the boxes below of the advantages and disadvantages of employing women from the *employer's* point of view.

Advantages	Disadvantages

You also wish to explain the advantages and disadvantages that there are for women considering secretarial work. Put your notes in the boxes below [on page 76].

Advantages	Disadvantages

2 **Listening, reading and writing** In each paper candidates are given 30 minutes to complete this section. All questions are compulsory. The recordings used are authentic and candidates are required to listen to the tape (sometimes once, sometimes twice) and select information to complete incomplete texts, select correct information from given choices, complete questionnaires, etc.

Example (Advanced)
You are going to listen to a short interview with a travel-writer, Arthur Lewis. You will hear an introduction first, and then the interview.

Imagine that after you have heard the interview a friend asks you about Arthur Lewis. The questions your friend asks you are written below, with space for your replies. You have 1 minute to read those questions now.

Now you will hear the interview *once*. As you listen you make notes in the spaces next to the questions. These notes will not be marked. When the interview is over, write your answers to the questions below.

a What sort of places has Arthur Lewis been to? (give 3 examples) ____________________ ____________________ *b* Why does he travel so much? __________	Use this space for rough notes if you want to

Results Scripts are marked either Pass (60%+) or Fail. First Class Pass (75%+) is awarded at Intermediate and Advanced levels only.

Weakness slips indicating which questions were inadequately answered are completed for candidates failing to obtain a pass grade.

Further information Available from PEI:
Regulations and syllabuses; *List of Most Commonly Misspelled Words*; specimen examination papers; examiners' reports for recent years and a complete specification of the 7 domains of language use.

Title

14.3 English for Office Skills

Conducted by Pitman Examinations Institute (PEI)
Godalming, Surrey GU7 1UU
Tel: Godalming (04868) 5311

Status

A single subject examination set at 2 levels.

A Pass at the Elementary level satisfies the English language requirement for PEI's Basic Commercial Group Certificate or Basic Secretarial Group Certificate. A Pass at the Intermediate level meets the requirement for the Commercial Group Certificate or the Secretarial Group Certificate. A First Class Pass at the Intermediate level meets the requirement for the Higher Commercial Certificate or the Higher Secretarial Group Certificate.

See Appendix 3 for Group Certificate requirements.

Aims

Designed to test elements of English language knowledge and skill required by young office workers. The Intermediate examination is intended to have a diagnostic purpose for employers.

Non-native speakers of English are advised to attempt these examinations when they have passed English as a Foreign Language (Intermediate) (see **14.2**) or reached an equivalent standard.

Levels

Elementary A lower level examination (see Appendix 2 for comparative levels) corresponding approximately to the lower level grades of CSE. Although no specialist knowledge is required, the skills tested are specific to those required in office work.

Intermediate An intermediate examination (see Appendix 2 for comparative levels), corresponding approximately to the higher grades of GCE O level. No specific business or commercial knowledge is required, but an understanding of typing conventions is assumed in the proof-reading question.

Availability

Available only through educational establishments registered as PEI examination centres (over 4000 worldwide). Examinations can be held at any time throughout the year at dates arranged by centres.

Content

Elementary (1 hour)

	Marks
7 separate objective tests to be worked individually to a fixed schedule.	
1 **Reading comprehension** A 300 word passage to be read with 10 multiple choice questions to be answered in 15 minutes.	20
2 **Listening comprehension** The invigilator reads 2 sets of instructions. The candidate is usually given 3 minutes to follow the first instruction and 5 the second instruction. The instructions can be to write a message, draw a map, etc.	15

Example

Listen to the following telephone message and write it out for your employer, Mr Smith:

'Ask Mr Smith to meet me tomorrow morning at 11 o'clock at the Plough Inn. This is Mr Brown speaking.'

3 **Spelling** 15 sentences read twice each with the word to be spelt repeated. (Words tested are from 120 chosen from PEI's List of Most Commonly Misspelled Words. Copies of the words to be tested available from PEI.) 15

4 **Punctuation** 2 or 3 sentences with punctuation marks omitted; sentences to be rewritten with punctuation inserted in 5 minutes. 10

5 **Grammar and syntax** 3 exercises to be completed in 10 minutes. 15

a correcting a grammatical error in each of 5 sentences.

Example
He don't like me.

b Inserting missing function words in a short passage.

Example
John is dependent . . . his parents, etc.

c Combining about 4 sentences into one.

Example
Mr Brown worked in a large office.
Mr Brown' secretary was called June.
The office was on the second floor.
The office was in a building.
The building was near the city centre.

6 **Vocabulary** 3 exercises to be completed in 9 minutes. 15

a Giving synonyms with the first letter provided.

Example
vanish d . . .

b Choosing the correct word from 2 given to complete a sentence.

Example
I shall certainly follow such valuable . . . (advice/advise)

c Selecting correct words from a choice given to complete a short passage.

7 **Proof-reading** 10 spelling or typographical errors to be identified (not corrected) in 10 minutes. 10

Example
if we sell enough Cars this year we should be able too expand next year, however, this is not allways the case etc.

Intermediate (1 hour)

9 separate tests to be worked individually to a fixed schedule.

1 **Reading comprehension** A 450–500 word passage to be read in 5 minutes; 20 multiple choice/short answer questions to be completed without looking back at the passage. 20

2 **Listening comprehension** Invigilator reads 150-word instructions from which a chart, map, diagram, form, etc must be constructed in 5 minutes; no note-taking permitted during reading.

Example
Your employer gives you the following instructions: I want you to draw up a new form which will be filled in by new employees. Give it a central heading *Personal Information Sheet* in capital letters. Draw a narrow left-hand margin. Write *Works No* at the top of this – nothing else. Now we want the following items of information from the employee: name, date of birth, home address, department, last employer. Give each item a number, etc.

Candidates may also be required to give short-form answers to questions based on a passage, providing facts or inferences.

3 **Spelling** 20 words (from PEI's list of most commonly misspelled words – other words may be introduced but no more than 2 in any one paper) read aloud in sentences by the invigilator to be spelt correctly. 20

4 **Punctuation** 2 or 3 sentences with 20 punctuation marks omitted; sentences to be rewritten with punctuation inserted in 5 minutes. 20

5 **Correctness** 20 sentences, each with a grammatical error to be identified and corrected in 10 minutes. 20

Example
We was hoping you would be different from the rest.

6 **Proof-reading** 15 spelling or typographical errors in a typescript to be identified but not corrected in 5 minutes. 15

Example
WHEN TO SELL YOUR CAr
More than 2000,000 use cars change hands in Britian every year.Private deals are beelieved to account for about 500,000 Vehicles a year. These cutout the . . . etc.

7 **Trap words** 10 sentences, each to be completed with the correct word from a choice of 2 or 3 in 3 minutes. 10

Example
. . . were a hundred people at the meeting. (There/Their)

8 **Vocabulary – selection and discrimination** Choosing the closest synonyms for 10 words from a choice in 5 minutes. 10

Example
acquire seize/obtain/steal/find

9 **Vocabulary – definitions** Choosing the correct words to match 10 definitions and initial letters in 5 minutes. 10

Example
Following tradition C. . . . .

Results At the Intermediate level, passes are awarded at 2 grades – Pass (60%) and First Class Pass (75%+). At the Elementary level scripts are marked Pass (60%+) or Fail. Weakness slips indicating which questions were inadequately answered are completed for candidates failing to reach a satisfactory standard.

Further information Available from PEI:
Regulations and syllabuses; *List of Most Commonly Misspelled Words*; specimen examination papers; examiners' reports for recent years.

Title

14.4 English for Business Communications

Conducted by Pitman Examinations Institute (PEI)
Godalming, Surrey GU7 1UU
Tel: Godalming (04868) 5311

Status Single-subject examination offered at 3 levels.
A Pass at Elementary meets the English language requirement for PEI's Basic Commercial and Basic Secretarial Group Certificates. A Pass at Intermediate meets the English language requirement for the Commercial and Secretarial Group Certificates. A Pass at Advanced meets the English language requirement for the Higher Commercial and Higher Secretarial Group Certificates.

Aims This examination is designed for native speakers but is taken by many overseas students. Overseas candidates are advised to reach the standard of English as a Foreign Language (Intermediate) or English Language (NCE) (Elementary) (see **14.2**) before attempting this examination. It aims to test the candidate's skill in using the language in business communications, especially the composition of suitable letters, memorandums and reports from information given, the use of sound commercial English, and knowledge of the conventional forms of layout for letters, memos, telegrams, telexes, reports and formal invitations. Candidates are expected to have a background knowledge of basic office organizations and personnel, of modern office equipment and staff working conditions.

Levels

Elementary An elementary examination requiring a knowledge of types and uses of business communication and ability to compose and lay out business letters.

Intermediate A higher-intermediate level examination requiring a general knowledge of business practice and the ability to analyse correspondence and assess the type of rcply needed.

Advanced An advanced level examination requiring a more profound knowledge of office duties and commerce. A fluent command of English is needed to enable the candidate to expand notes adding necessary details to provide authentic answers.

See Appendix 2 for comparative levels of ESP examinations.

Availability

Available only through educational establishments registered as PEI examination centres (over 4000 worldwide). Examinations can be held at any time of the year at dates arranged by centres.

Content

Elementary (2 hours)

The examination is in 2 parts: *Marks*

Part 1 A short objective test which is compulsory, on the correct choice of medium of communication and layout. 20

Example

Read through the following passage and fill in the spaces appropriately.

Letters may be divided into three general classes: p . . ., b . . . and o . . . The reference on a letter may consist merely of the i . . . of the w . . . and the typist, or refer to a d . . . file number. The reference is to identify the p . . . or department sending the letter. The date on a letter should not be a . . . and should appear in the order d . . ., m . . ., y . . .. When it is necesary to indicate that a particular letter is of a confidential nature, the word c . . . should be written . . ..

Part II One compulsory question (a letter) and three other questions from a choice of 5. Candidates are expected to be able to write letters from notes, compose personal letters, formal invitations, replies, memoranda, international telegrams, telexes and other business messages. Each question carries 20 marks. 80

Example

Write a memorandum from the Chief Cashier to the Company Secretary suggesting that he sends a circular letter to customers who are failing to pay their accounts within 28 days. Say that permission must bc given before customers can extend their period of credit. For amounts over £100 discount will be withheld if cheques are not received within 28 days.

Intermediate (2½ hours)

Two compulsory questions, one a letter and one a report, and 3 others from a choice of 5. Candidates are expected to be able to deal with the types of communication covered in Elementary as well as writing personal letters for employers, including letters of introduction and recommendation; letters of welcome, congratulations, etc; telephone messages; advertisements; and reports.

Example
You are in charge of the petty cash which is kept on the imprest 16
system, the imprest or float of £50 being restored at the end of each month. Last month the balance was very small and you consider that the imprest will soon not meet the overall monthly expenditure.

Prepare a report for the Chief Cashier requesting this increase (suggest required amount); state where the largest expenditure increase was and suggest one method by which this rate of increase could be reduced.

Advanced (3 hours)

Five questions, 3 compulsory: a letter, a report and composition of a short text, eg a telegram, an advertisement, or notice, plus 2 other questions from a choice of 4. At the advanced level a higher standard of composition is expected and the matters dealt with relate to a wider range of business undertakings. Each question carries 20 marks.

Example
You work as the Chief Cashier and have been asked to investigate a 20
Rail Account Order Scheme for use by the staff.

You have ascertained that £100 deposit is payable; the railway authority issues members with Rail Account Order Books; one order is issued for each journey; an employee presents this order at the ticket office and the firm is sent a monthly account for settlement within 7 days. You have obtained a leaflet setting out the Scheme in full.

Write a report to the Chief Financial Controller, making recommendations for the Scheme to be brought into use.

Results Scripts are marked Pass (60%+) or Fail. First Class Pass (75%+) is awarded at Intermediate and Advanced levels only. Weakness slips indicating which areas of a candidates performance were inadequate are completed for all candidates failing to reach a satisfactory standard. See **14.1**.

Further information

14.5 English for the Secretary

Title

Conducted by
Pitman Examinations Institute (PEI)
Godalming, Surrey GU7 1UU
Tel: Godalming (04868) 5311

Status
Single-subject examination offered at one level.
A Pass meets the English language requirement for PEI's Higher Secretarial Group Certificate.

Aims
This examination aims to test the secretary's ability to deal with the types of communications met in an office. It is recommended that candidates should be practising secretaries and/or have studied secretarial practice.

Level
An advanced level examination of approximately the same standard as English for Business Communications (Advanced) (see **14.4**). Candidates should have reached the standard of GCE O level before attempting this examination.

See Appendix 2 for comparative levels of ESP examinations.

Availability
Available only through educational establishments registered as PEI examination centres (over 4000 worldwide). Examinations can be held at any time of the year at dates arranged by centres.

Content
Time: 3 hours
Candidates are given 6 linked tasks in which they must act as secretary to a particular person. Candidates are expected to use their own knowledge to add the necessary details to produce comprehensive and authentic answers. All questions are compulsory and can cover: letters, memoranda, international telegrams, telexes, telemessages, telephone messages, summaries, reports, agendas and minutes of meetings.

Marks

Example 15

You work as Secretary to Mr J Phillips, the Managing Director of Phillips Industries Ltd, 44 High Street, Kew, London TW6 1LD. Mr Phillips has been called away on business suddenly and has left you the following instructions. Please complete the exercises in any order you wish. All exercises must be attempted. Invent names, addresses as appropriate. The reference number for all correspondence is JP/your initials.

1 Mr Phillips had an appointment at 11 am with Mr J Johnson at his offices in Green Street, London SW1A 3BW. Please telephone Mr Johnson to apologize for Mr Phillips' absence and make an

alternative appointment. Write a confirmatory letter giving the date and time of the new appointment.

Results Scripts are marked First Class Pass (75%+), Pass (60%+) or Fail. Weakness slips indicating which areas of a candidate's performance were inadequate are completed for all candidates failing to reach a satisfactory standard.

Further information See **14.1**.

15 Royal Society of Arts Examinations Board (RSA)

15.1 English as a Foreign Language

Title

Conducted by
The Royal Society of Arts Examinations Board
John Adam Street, Adelphi, London WC2N 6EZ
Tel: London (01) 839 1691

Status
A single-subject examination set at 3 levels.

Aims
This examination is intended for those learning English as a foreign language, particularly those studying in the UK.

Stage I Will test ability to use the language as a medium of immediate communication – to deal aurally and orally with the basic situations of everyday life; and the ability to read, write and understand written communications of a non-specific nature appropriate to adult candidates.

Stage II Will test ability to use the language to express and to understand simple connected thought, narration, description and hypothesis orally and in writing.

Stage III Will test ability to use the language to express, describe and discuss the candidate's own ideas and those of others.

Levels
Stage I A lower level examination set at a standard below that of Cambridge First Certificate.

Stage II An intermediate examination set at a level roughly equivalent to Cambridge First Certificate.

Stage III A more advanced examination set at a level roughly equivalent to or slightly more difficult than Cambridge Proficiency.

Availability
Available only through approved RSA examination centres in the UK and overseas. Where there are no RSA centres the British Council is often willing to provide facilities. Candidates of any age may enter, but may sit *for only one Stage at a time*. Examinations are held 4 times a year: in March, May, June and November. The examination is also available on a Mode 3 basis which can be used to provide examinations on dates other than those in the timetable, or examinations for specific purposes based on syllabuses provided by centres.

Content
The format for the 3 Stages is similar:

Part I Grammar (30 minutes)

A 40-item objective test of a range of language items. The items make up a narrative when read together.
Stage I The items are based on a series of pictures.

Example
It's eleven o'clock . . . *a* at the morning
b in the morning
c of the morning
d the morning

Stage II As for Stage I.
Stage III The items are based on a printed passage.

Example
Mr Kemp took his briefcase with him . . . he could refer to his notes.
a so as that
b in case
c providing
d in order that

Part II Reading Comprehension and Composition (2 hours)

Reading Comprehension Passage(s) printed on the question paper, with 5 questions based on each passage. Candidates must answer each question in not more than one sentence.
Stage I One passage of about 250 words.
Stage II 2 passages, each of about 150 words.
Stage III 3 passages, each of 150–200 words.

Composition Composition subjects are chosen from the following:

a narrative or dialogue based on a given outline.
b an account of an everyday situation based on material supplied (eg in the form of a series of pictures).
c letter-writing in a given situation.

Stage I 2 compositions, each of 100–120 words.

Example
Write a letter to an accommodation agency in Great Britain or your own country asking for help in finding somewhere to live. Mention the price you want to pay, the place, the kind of house or flat. You should set the letter out correctly.

Stage II 2 compositions, each of 120–150 words.

Example

Imagine that you recently witnessed a robbery, an accident, an unidentified flying object, or some other unusual happening. Write a report for the police or other appropriate authorities of what you saw. Make your account as clear and factual as possible.

Stage III 2 compositions, each of 180–220 words.

Example

You have been asked to write a review for your college magazine of a play recently performed by the Drama Society. You should include comments on the actors, on the staging and other technical aspects of the production. You should also make some mention of the work which was done by the helpers, and say something about the reaction of the audience.

Part III Oral/Aural Test

Aural Comprehension A passage is read aloud to the candidates twice. Notes may be taken during the second reading. Five questions based on the passage are printed on the question paper. Candidates must answer each one in not more than one sentence.

Stage I A short passage written in current English.

Stage II A passage of about 300 words. Greater emphasis is given to deduction and inference in questions.

Stage III A passage of about 300 words which may be more technical or abstract.

Conversation

Stage I Directed questioning to the candidate, including questions on some visual material provided. Candidates are expected to use a range of tenses and adapt answers to questioning.

Stage II The form of the test is similar to that for Stage I but candidates will be expected to show greater fluency, greater control of sounds, stress, rhythm and intonation, and some descriptive ability.

Stage III Candidates must read aloud a passage given to them shortly before the test begins and sustain a conversation about the passage and other topics.

Results

Passes are awarded at 3 grades – Pass, Pass with Credit and Pass with Distinction.

Further information

Available from the Royal Society of Arts (Publications), Murray Road, Orpington, Kent BR5 3RB:

Past papers; syllabus and regulations, English as a Foreign Language; *Reports on Examinations, Part II, Single-Subject Examinations.*

Title **15.2 Communicative use of English as a Foreign Language**

Conducted by The Royal Society of Arts Examinations Board
John Adam Street, Adelphi, London WC2N 6EZ
Tel: London (01) 839 1691

Status A unit-credit examination set at 3 levels.

Aims The examinations are designed for overseas students living, working or studying in the UK, or intending to visit the country on a long- or short-term basis. The language skills tested are those of 'in-Britain' English.

Level The 3 levels are not intended to correspond to other Stage I, II and III examinations offered by the RSA. Levels are defined internally. No information on equivalences is available.

Availability The examinations are available only through approved RSA examination centres in the UK and overseas. Examinations are held twice a year, in late May and late November.
No restriction in terms of age is imposed on entry, but the audience envisaged is adult. Candidates are free to enter any combination of the component tests at any combination of levels, except that the same test may not be attempted at more than one level at each examination sitting.

Content The examination is available at 3 levels: Basic, Intermediate and Advanced. At each level the examination consists of 4 tests: Reading, Listening, Writing and Oral Interaction.

Test 1 Reading (Time: All levels – 1 hour)

Candidates are provided with source material in the form of authentic documents which provide the basis of the operations and tasks to be carried out. Documents may consist of the following text types:

Basic forms, guides, advertisements, letters, postcards, sets of instructions, diary entries, timetables, maps, plans
Intermediate newspaper reports, features, telegrams
Advanced extracts from novels, poems, newspaper editorials

A number of short-form or objective questions follow each document.

Examples from the Basic level
You would like to see more of Britain and have decided to spend a weekend in Cornwall. Here are some pages from 2 tourist booklets about the West Country (supplied to candidates). Look through the booklet for a few minutes.

You want to see as much as possible during your weekend and so look at the '*Places to Visit*' at the front of the booklet.

1 Are the following places open on Sundays between October and March? Write YES or NO in the answer column.

a Barbara Hepworth Museum ☐
b County Demonstration Garden ☐
c Launceston Castle ☐

You decide to stay in Penzance and to make some visits from there. Read the list of 'Serviced Accommodation'. In the appropriate columns below put a cross (X) if the answer is YES.

	Carnson Guest House	Estoril Private Hotel	Kilindi Private Hotel
2 Is it close to the station?			
3 Does it have 'central heating'?			
4 Does it have a colour TV lounge?			
5 Is there a service charge?			
6 How much is off-season bed and breakfast per day?			

Test 2 Listening (Time: All levels – 25–30 minutes)

Candidates are provided with taped source material which takes the form of authentic or semi-authentic texts of the following types:

Basic monologue, dialogue, announcement, interview, song
Intermediate as for Basic, plus lecture, discussion, documentary, social interaction
Advanced as for Intermediate, plus multi-participant interaction, anecdote, sketch, commentary

These texts provide the basis for a range of questions:

Basic candidates are given the opportunity to study questions before they listen to the text.
Intermediate a combination of pre- and post-listening questions.
Advanced a combination of pre- and post-listening questions but post-listening questions predominate.

Examples from the Basic level
You are going to listen to a taped magazine programme and answer questions.

1 What is the name of the instrument used in villages to tell the time before they had clocks?
a sunbox
b sundial
c sunclock
d sunsail

2 Fill in the gaps.
There were about . . . railways in Britain in . . . when they decided to introduce a standard . . . across the . . .

3 Your plan is to travel from London to Bristol in an Inter-City train next Tuesday. Next Tuesday for you with your plan there will be:

a No problem ☐ *b* Very few trains ☐ *c* No trains at all ☐

Test 3 Writing (Time: Basic – 1 hour; Intermediate – 1½ hours; Advanced – 2 hours)

Questions are set requiring the candidate to produce samples of writing of the following types:

Basic letter, postcard, note, forms
Intermediate as for Basic, plus guide, set of instructions
Advanced as for Intermediate, plus newspaper report, set of notes

Example from the Basic level
A friend has invited you to stay with him/her while you are looking for somewhere to live. You now think you will probably be able to find your own accommodation very quickly through an accommodation agency and will not need your friend's help.

Thank your friend for his/her offer. Explain what has happened and apologize for any trouble caused. Tell your friend you'll contact him/her as soon as you have moved into your new home.

Write your note and your friend's address on the postcard below.

Test 4 Oral Interaction (Time: All levels – approximately 15 minutes)

The form of the test is the same at each level. The test is divided into three parts, each observed by an assessor nominated by the RSA. Interactions are normally face-to-face but telephone conversations are not excluded. Some role play is required, but candidates are not asked to assume specialized or fantasy roles.

1 Interaction between the candidate and an interlocutor (normally a teacher known to the candidate).

Example from the Basic level
A local club has invited you to give a talk to a group of visitors to the town

or region where you live, giving them as much information as possible. You have asked a teacher to give you some ideas for your talk and you have been given the following suggestions. You may, of course, add some more of your own:

areas of natural beauty	climate
entertainment	shops
opportunities for sport	industry
local food	health facilities
local customs	education
housing	

In a few minutes, a teacher will ask you to tell him/her as much as you can about your home town or region.

2 Interaction between candidates in pairs or threes without the interlocutor.

Example from the Basic level
You and your partner are travelling in an air balloon. You each have a bag containing some valuable personal items (list of contents supplied to candidates) but the pilot has told you that the balloon is too heavy and you must throw your bags out. You may, however, each keep 2 of the items. Find out from your partner what he/she has in his/her bag and discuss what items each of you wants to keep. Be prepared to give reasons for your choice.

3 Report from the candidates to the interlocutor on the interaction in Part 2.

Results

Candidates are graded Pass or Fail for each test taken.

Further information

Available from the Royal Society of Arts Examinations Board (Publications), Murray Road, Orpington, Kent BR5 3RB:
Syllabus and regulations – Examinations in the Communicative Use of English as a Foreign Language and English as a Foreign Language; past papers and tapes.

16 Trinity College, London

Title 16.1 Spoken English as a Foreign or Second Language

Conducted by Trinity College, London
11–13 Mandeville Place, London W1M 6AQ
Tel: London (01) 935 5773

Status Single-subject examinations set at 12 grades. Regarded by the British Council as comprising a useful series of graded tests in oral communicative ability.

Aims To cater for all levels of achievement from elementary to very advanced. The main emphasis is on oral communication – the understanding of spoken English and the ability to speak it communicatively.

Levels Examinations are held at 12 grades. The grades progress in reasonably equal steps from Grade 1 for beginners to Grade 12 for advanced students. The requirements are cumulative, so that a candidate must be familiar with everything in the syllabuses of lower grades before moving to a higher grade.

Grades 1–3 beginners
Grades 4–5 lower intermediate
Grades 6–9 intermediate
Grade 10 (Lower Proficiency) set at a level approximately equivalent to Cambridge First Crtificate as far as conversational ability is concerned.
Grade 11 (Proficiency) set at a level approximately equivalent to Cambridge Proficiency as far as conversational ability is concerned.
Grade 12 (Higher Proficiency) set at a level approximately equivalent to the Cambridge Diploma as far as conversational ability is concerned.
See Appendix 1 for comparative levels of EFL examinations.

Availability Entry is not open to those who speak English as a native language. Candidates below the age of 7 are ineligible; adults are recommended not to enter below Grades 3 or 4. Available only through registered centres in the UK, Europe, the Middle East, Sri Lanka, Japan, South East Asia, Australia, New Zealand, South America and South Africa. In the UK examinations are held on dates arranged at the mutual convenience of the College and the centre. Outside the UK, examinations, which are conducted by examiners sent from the UK, are arranged as conveniently as possible within the itineraries of examining tours; wherever possible, the centre's preferred dates are used. Entry forms should be sent to local representatives. Entry forms for the London centre may be sent direct to Trinity College.

Content

Grade 1 (5 minutes)

An interview, including appropriate exchanges of everyday greetings and courtesies, responses to very simple commands and answers to short questions. Candidates should be familiar with the days of the week, months of the year and the seasons, and be able to use a few adjectives of size and colour.

Grade 2 (6 minutes)

An interview including a test of familiarity with certain prepositions, requests to perform certain actions, eg cleaning one's teeth, brushing one's hair, etc, and questions about pictures ('What is he/she doing?' 'Is he/she washing his/her face?' 'Are they playing tennis?' etc).

Grade 3 (7 minutes)

An interview in which the candidate is expected not only to answer questions and obey commands, but also to put questions and give commands to the examiner.

Grade 4 (8 minutes)

	Marks
a The candidate studies a short unprepared passage for about 8 minutes and then tells the examiner in some detail what it is about.	30%
b Conversation with the examiner: including suggestions, requests, and accepting and refusing offers or invitations.	70%

Grade 5 (10 minutes)

a The candidate studies a short unprepared passage for about	30%

8 minutes and then tells the examiner in some detail what it is about.

b Conversation with the examiner: The candidate should not merely answer the examiner's questions but ask questions and make comments. 70%

Grades 6–9 (Grades 6 and 7: 12 minutes; Grade 8: 15 minutes; Grade 9: 20 minutes)

a The candidate studies a passage of dialogue before entering the examination room and then speaks one of the roles in the dialogue; what is said by one speaker in the dialogue is left blank. The candidate supplies appropriate speech for this blank role when speaking the dialogue with the examiner. 20%

b The candidate studies a book and discusses its plot and characters with the examiner. 30%

c Conversation with the examiner: The subject matter may arise from the prepared book, or may be related to the candidate's daily life or to any of his interests. 50%

Grade 10 (Lower Proficiency) (20 minutes)

a The candidate studies a passage of dialogue before entering the examination room. What is said by one of the speakers has been left blank. The candidate supplies the appropriate speech for this blank role when speaking the dialogue with the examiner. 20%

b The candidate studies 2 books and discusses them with the examiner. 30%

c The candidate delivers a prepared talk lasting about 3 minutes on some aspect of his studies or occupation or some more general topic. Notes may be used. Candidates under 18 may tell a story lasting about three minutes. 20%

d Conversation with the examiner. 30%

Grade 11 Proficiency (25 minutes, excluding section *e*)

a The candidate retells a passage or story of about 250–300 words read aloud once by the examiner and then answers questions about it. Notes may be taken. 15%

b The candidate studies 2 books and discusses them with the examiner. 30%

c The candidate delivers a 3–4 minute prepared talk on some aspect of his studies or occupation or on some more general topic. Notes may be used. Candidates under 18 may tell a story lasting 3–4 minutes. 15%

d Conversation with the examiner: part of the conversation may be on matters arising from the prepared talk. 30%

e The candidate retells in writing a passage of about 300 words read aloud twice by the examiner. Notes may be taken. 20 minutes are allowed for the writing. 10%

Grade 12 Higher Proficiency (30 minutes, excluding section *e*)

a The candidate retells a passage or story of about 300 words read aloud once by the examiner and then answers questions about it. Notes may be taken. 15%

b The candidate studies 3 books for discussion with the examiner. 30%

c The candidate delivers a prepared talk lasting 4–5 minutes on some aspect of his studies or occupation or on some more general topic. Candidates under 18 may tell a story lasting 4–5 minutes. Notes may be used. 15%

d Conversation with the examiner: Part of this conversation may be on matters arising from the prepared talk. 30%

e The candidate retells in writing a passage of about 300 words read aloud once by the examiner. Notes may be taken. 30 minutes are allowed for the writing. 10%

Results

Certificates are awarded to successful candidates for each Grade. The following marks must be obtained: for a Pass Certificate, 65%; for a Pass with Merit Certificate, 75%; and for an Honours Certificate, 85%.

Certificates are normally sent to successful candidates within 6 weeks. An assessment form is completed by the examiner for each candidate and distributed to candidates as soon as possible after the examination session.

Further information

Available from Trinity College London:
Examination syllabus – Spoken English as a Foreign or Second Language; specimen comprehension passages.

Title

16.2 Written English (Intermediate)

Conducted by Trinity College London
11–13 Mandeville Place, London W1M 6AQ
Tel: London (01) 935 5773

Status Single-subject examination.

Aims To give entrants an opportunity of showing that their command of English is not limited to the oral medium but extends to the printed and written medium.

Level Corresponding roughly to Grade 9 of Trinity College's examinations in Spoken English as a Foreign or Second Language. (See Appendix 1.)

Availability Available only through registered centres in the UK, Europe, the Middle East, Sri Lanka, Japan, South East Asia, Australia, New Zealand, South America and South Africa. The examination is held twice a year, in May/June and November/December. Entry forms should be sent to local representatives. Entry forms for the London centre may be sent direct to Trinity College.

Content Time: 3 hours

1 **Reading Comprehension** Reading a passage of about 200 words and then completing and answering a number of free-response questions in complete sentences.
2 **Cloze test** Completing a passage of about 300 words from which words have been omitted. Candidates choose the best of 3 suggested words to insert in each gap.
3 **Grammar** Completing 10 sentences in which gaps have been left. Cues may be given.

Examples
Do I have to buy a ticket? No, you . . . if you don't want to.
How I wish she would stop . . . (talk).

4 **Composition** Writing a composition or dialogue of about 350 words. There is a choice of topic.

Examples
Write a dialogue between two people discussing ONE of the following topics:

a Where to go for their holidays.
b What to buy a friend for his or her birthday.
c Their favourite season of the year.

Results The following marks must be obtained for the award of a Certificate: for a Pass Certificate, 65%; for a Pass with Merit Certificate, 75%; and for an Honours Certificate, 85%.

Further information Available from Trinity College London:
Examination syllabus – Written English (Intermediate); copies of previous sessions' examination papers.

17 University of Cambridge Local Examinations Syndicate (Cambridge)

17.1 Preliminary English Test (PET)

Title

Conducted by University of Cambridge Local Examinations Syndicate (Cambridge)
Syndicate Buildings, 1 Hills Road, Cambridge CB1 2EU
Tel: Cambridge (0223) 61111

Status A single-subject examination.

Aims To provide a general English proficiency examination.

Level An elementary examination (see Appendix 1) representing about 350 hours from beginner level and testing appropriate oral and written skills.

Availability By arrangement between schools, colleges, course organizers, etc and the Syndicate. Taken on varying dates within 4 testing periods in March, May, July–August and November.

Content The total time for the test is just over 2 hours. The test has the following 8 sections:

1 Multiple-choice vocabulary and usage items

Example
I can't do the exercise because I've . . . my book at home.
a let *b* forgotten *c* taken *d* left *e* sent

2 Blank-filling to test structures and usage

Example
Excuse me, that book is . . .. It . . . my name on it.

3 & 4 Guided compositions

Example
Policeman: Now, you say you saw the accident. Can you tell me what happened?
Yourself: Yes. I was standing on the corner, waiting to cross the road . . .

5 & 6 Multiple-choice items on situations and an extended text (recorded).

7 & 8 Interview, consisting of sets of standard questions and a short role-playing exercise.

Results A pass–fail list is issued to centres, and a result slip is provided for successful candidates. 50% of the marks are allotted to the written (1–4) sections, and 50% to the oral (5–8) sections.

Further information A specimen paper, regulations with details of entry procedure and current fees, and application forms for registration of centres are available from the Syndicate.

Title

17.2 First Certificate in English (FCE)

Conducted by University of Cambridge Local Examinations Syndicate (Cambridge)
(in association with the British Council)
Syndicate Buildings, 1 Hills Road, Cambridge CB1 2EU
Tel: Cambridge (0223) 61111

Status A single-subject examination with wide acceptance for commercial and preliminary academic purposes.

Aims To provide a comprehensive general English proficiency examination.

Level An intermediate examination requiring a knowledge of all language skills (see Appendix 1 for comparative levels).

Availability Candidates, who must be of other than English mother tongue, must enter through a recognized centre. Examinations are held in June and December. Last dates for entry are 23 March for June, and 9 October for December (earlier for centres outside the UK).

Content From June 1984 there are 5 papers:

Paper 1 Reading comprehension (1 hour)

This is a multiple-choice test divided into Sections A and B. Section A has 25 incomplete sentences followed by 4 words or phrases, one of which is appropriate to complete each sentence. The sentences are designed to test knowledge of vocabulary, usage and formal grammatical control.

Example
After a lot of difficulty, he . . . to open the door.
a managed *b* succeeded *c* obtained *d* realized

Section B has 15 multiple-choice questions, based on 2 or more passages or documents. Each item is in the form of a question or incomplete sentence followed by a choice of 4 suggested answers or completions, to test comprehension of gist or detailed content.

Paper 2 Composition ($1\frac{1}{2}$ hours)

Candidates must write on 2 subjects in 120–180 words each from a choice which will include narrative, discussion, a letter, description, a speech or a subject based on prepared reading. For the latter a choice of 3 texts is given (for example, Shaw's *Arms and the Man*, Dickens' *Nicholas Nickleby*, Bennett's *The Card*) as specified in the Regulations.

Paper 3 Use of English (2 hours)

This paper has 2 sections. Section A may include:

a modified cloze
b rewriting sentences using different constructions
c producing the correct part of speech using a given root word
d writing out a passage in dialogue form
e sentence completion or formation
f a vocabulary test

Section B is a standard composition task involving information retrieval with a realistic background.

Example
Below is an advertisement for a job which appeared in a newspaper and the notes made on 4 people who applied for the job and were interviewed. Using the information given, continue in about 50 words each of the 4 paragraphs, giving your reasons for choosing each candidate for the job.

Paper 4 Listening comprehension (30 minutes)

Questions of various types, including multiple-choice, based on a recorded series of texts such as radio-type sequences of news or features, situational dialogues, announcements, etc.

Paper 5 Interview (Approximately 20 minutes)

The interview consists of 3 parts:

a The examiner shows the candidate a photograph and asks specific questions about the scene, and then on generally related topics to develop a short conversation.

b The candidate is handed a short passage and given a few moments to look through it. He is then asked to identify the probable speech situation and asked to read it aloud.

c This part consists of communicative exercises of varying types, including role play, discussion and problem solving. This part of the test may be taken with a group of 3 candidates.

Example

The examiner outlines as a situation an airport information desk where a flight has been seriously delayed, and elicits by means of spoken or written prompts, specific questions and comments about:

The next flight
Hotel for the night – and who pays for this
Contacting waiting relations, etc.

Results Certificates are awarded in 3 grades, A, B and C, which are based on the aggregate of the marks gained in the 5 papers. There are 2 failing grades, D and E. Results of individual papers are not issued. It is not possible to retake single papers. Two-thirds of the marks are allocated to papers 1, 2 and 3, and the remaining one-third to papers 4 and 5.

Further information Optional papers are available at this level (see **17.5, 17.6, 17.8**). A list of centres, regulations, an introductory booklet with specimen material (including a cassette recording of the Listening Comprehension Test), and details of current fees are available from local centres or direct from Cambridge.

Title

17.3 Certificate of Proficiency in English (CPE)

Conducted by University of Cambridge Local Examinations Syndicate (Cambridge) (in association with the British Council)
Syndicate Buildings, 1 Hills Road, Cambridge CB1 2EU
Tel: Cambridge (0223) 61111

Status A single-subject examination recognized by British universities and other institutions as a matriculation or entrance requirement in English language in line with GCE O level English language. Outside the UK it is recognized by a number of governments as part of the qualification for teaching English in primary and secondary schools.

Aims To provide a comprehensive general English proficiency examination of an advanced standard.

Level An advanced examination requiring a knowledge of all language skills (see Appendix 1 for comparative levels).

Candidates, who must be of other than English mother tongue, must enter through a recognized centre. Examinations are held in June and December. Last dates for entry 23 March for June and 9 October for December (earlier for centres outside the UK). **Availability**

From June 1984 there are 5 papers: **Content**

Paper 1 Reading comprehension (1 hour)

This is a multiple-choice test divided into Sections A and B. Section A has 25 incomplete sentences each followed by 5 words or phrases, one of which is appropriate to complete each sentence. The sentences are designed to test knowledge of vocabulary, usage and formal grammatical control.

Example
He couldn't . . . his father that he was telling the truth.
a admit *b* confide *c* trust *d* convince

Section B has 15 multiple-choice questions based on 2 or more passages. Each item is in the form of a question or incomplete sentence followed by 4 suggested answers or completions to test comprehension of gist or detailed content, or communicative factors such as nuance, register or stylistic effects as these reveal the intention of the writer.

Paper 2 Composition (2 hours)

Candidates must write 2 compositions from a choice of descriptive, situational or discursive topics, or topics based on prepared reading. For the prepared reading, a choice of three texts is given (for example, Scott Fitzgerald's *The Great Gatsby*) as specified in the Regulations.

Examples
Write a descriptive account of a visit to a crowded beach. (350 words)
Write a balanced discussion on the theme 'A woman's place is in the home'. You may write in the form of a dialogue between 2 speakers or in essay form. (200 words)
Hardy: *Far from the Madding Crowd*
What underlying view of life do you find in this book, and how is it expressed? (350 words)

Paper 3 Use of English (2 hours)

The paper is divided into 2 sections:

Section A Open-completion items designed to test control of the patterns and usage of English, and the ability to manipulate the language at clause and sentence level.

Examples
Although the team played well, they lost.
Despite . . . .
He took his car to the garage . . . it repaired.

Section B Open-ended comprehension questions and summary exercises based on a reading passage.

Paper 4 Listening comprehension (30 minutes)

Questions of various types, including multiple-choice, based on a recorded series of texts such as radio-type sequences of news or features, situational dialogues, announcements, etc.

Paper 5 Interview (Approximately 20 minutes)

The interview consists of 3 parts:

a The examiner shows the candidate a photograph and asks specific questions about the scene and then on generally related topics to develop a short conversation.

b The candidate is handed a short passage and given a few moments to look through it. He is then asked to identify the probable speech situation and asked to read it aloud.

c This part consists of communicative exercises of varying types, including role play, discussion and problem solving. This part of the test may be taken with a group of 3 candidates.

Example
The examiner initiates a discussion on the varying purposes and levels of education, inviting concrete reference, eg:

a tribesman in an industrializing country
someone engaged in negotiation work at any level
a science student.

Results

Certificates are awarded at 3 grades: A, B and C, which are based on the aggregate of marks gained in the 5 papers. There are 2 failing grades: D and E. Results of individual papers are not issued, and it is not possible to retake single papers. Two-thirds of the marks are allocated to papers 1, 2 and 3, and the remaining one-third to papers 4 and 5.

Further information

Optional papers are available at this level (see **17.7** and **17.8**). A list of centres, regulations, an introductory booklet with specimen material (including a cassette recording of the Listening Comprehension Test) and details of current fees are available from local centres or direct from Cambridge.

Title

17.4 Diploma of English Studies (DES)

Conducted by

University of Cambridge Local Examinations Syndicate (Cambridge) (in association with the British Council)
Syndicate Buildings, 1 Hills Road, Cambridge CB1 2EU
Tel: Cambridge (0223) 61111

Status

A unit-credit examination, ie papers do not all have to be taken at the same sitting.

Aims

To provide an advanced qualification in English language, English literature, and associated aspects of British life, history and culture for non-native speakers.

Level

The standard is intended to be comparable with that of the first part of a university degree course in English and its literature in the UK. (See Appendix 1 for comparative levels of EFL examinations.)

Availability

Candidates, who must be non-native speakers, must enter through recognized centres, not all of which can accept entries for the Diploma. The examination is held in June only. The last date for entry is 23 March (earlier for centres outside the UK).

Candidates must possess, usually on entry, a Certificate of Proficiency (see **17.3**) at Grade A or B.

One or more individual papers may be taken each year. The Diploma is awarded on the previous Proficiency performance and performance in the following papers:

Content

Language and appreciation (3 hours)

This paper tests candidates' ability to express ideas and show critical appreciation in a mature and effective way. Three questions are set.

Literature (3 papers to be chosen, or 2 with the Life and Institutions paper) (3 hours)

Candidates are required to answer 3 questions, at least one from each of 2 sections. Texts or authors are normally prescribed for 2 consecutive years. Lists are given in the Syndicate's Regulations for Examinations in English as a Foreign Language and an advance list for the examinations 3 years ahead can be obtained.

Examples

Literature A	*Section I*	Shakespeare (two prescribed plays)
	Section II	Ben Jonson, The Metaphysical Poets, Richardson (*Pamela*)
Literature B	*Section I*	Cowper and Clare, Shelley, Thackeray (*Vanity Fair*)
	Section II	Browning, George Eliot (*Middlemarch*), Yeats (writings to 1919)
Literature C	*Section I*	D H Lawrence (*The Plumed Serpent* or *Kangaroo*), E M Forster, T S Eliot (poems)
	Section II	W H Auden, Henry Green, Tom Stoppard

The marking is based on an ability to illustrate general arguments by detailed reference to the texts read, and for the ability to relate detailed study of a particular author or text to background knowledge of the period of study. Where texts are not given, candidates have a free choice, but they should know in detail a representative sample of the author's work, including at least 2 novels/plays or a comparable selection of poetry or prose as appropriate.

Life and institutions (3 hours)

Candidates must answer 3 questions on 2 of the 5 topics prescribed.

Examples of topics

British urban development since 1920
The making of the welfare state
The legal profession in Britain
The position of women in British society since 1700
Britain and Ireland

Credit is given for breadth and depth of study, and for some ability to relate the chosen topic to British history and culture in general.

Results The Diploma is awarded in the following grades:

First Grade – outstanding
Second Grade – Upper Division – very good
– Lower Division – good
Third Grade – pass

Further information An optional additional test is available in Translation at this level (see **17.8**). *Information Leaflet 8/1/E*, a list of centres, regulations, past question papers, reports and details of current fees are available from local centres or direct from Cambridge.

17.5 English for Business (First Certificate in English)

Title

Conducted by University of Cambridge Local Examinations Syndicate (Cambridge)
Syndicate Buildings, 1 Hills Road, Cambridge CB1 2EU
Tel: Cambridge (0223) 61111

Status Optional additional paper which can be taken only if the candidate has successfully taken or is taking the First Certificate examination (see 17.2).

Aims The paper is intended to provide a qualification in some language skills needed in the study or practice of commerce.

Level A special purpose examination at post First Certificate level (see Appendix 2 for comparative levels of ESP examinations).

Availability As for the main First Certificate examination as specified in the Regulations for each year, subject to availability at particular centres (see 17.2).

Content There is one 2-hour paper with 4 questions:

1 A 300-word passage on a business topic, with a variety of open-ended, multiple-choice or summarizing questions. The following extract gives some idea of the nature and level of the passages:

> A large number of shops in many countries still consist of small unit establishments. In form the bulk of them are sole traders (one-man businesses). The figures concerning these could be a little misleading. They constitute a majority of the total number of shops and they account for a large proportion of the total turnover . . .

2 A passage on a business topic with blanks to be filled with a suitable word.

Example
The really gifted and successful entrepreneur, or business man is . . . 1 one who can pick out, among all the uncertainties . . . 2 his business . . .

3 A letter on a business theme, usually including the giving of a letterhead and address.

Example
An English firm wishes to place an order with you for a product in your country. Write a letter describing what you can offer and quoting prices and methods of delivery.

4 Figures and abbreviations are given which have to be written out in the form in which they would be spoken over the telephone.

Example
$54\frac{1}{2}$%   24.05 hrs   2,650

Results Successful candidates are awarded endorsements in 3 grades: A, B and C. There are 2 failing grades: D and E.

A successful result in an optional examination at which the candidate is unsuccessful in the main First Certificate examination will be held over by the Syndicate until the candidate qualifies on a later occasion.

Further information As for the main examination (see **17.2**). A specimen paper is also available.

Title

17.6 English for Science (First Certificate in English)

Conducted by University of Cambridge Local Examinations Syndicate (Cambridge)
Syndicate Buildings, 1 Hills Road, Cambridge CB1 2EU
Tel: Cambridge (0223) 61111

Status Optional additional paper which can be taken only if the candidate has successfully taken or is taking the First Certificate examination (see **17.2**).

Aims The paper is intended to provide a qualification in some language skills needed for scientific study.

Level A special purpose examination at post First Certificate level (see Appendix 2 for comparative levels of ESP examinations).

Availability As for the main First Certificate examination as specified in the Regulations for each year, subject to availability at particular centres (see **17.2**).

Content There is one 2-hour paper with 4 questions:

1 and 2 Passages of a general scientific nature, with a variety of open-ended, multiple choice and summarizing questions. The following extract gives some idea of the nature and level of the passages:

> Steel is made from pig iron by removing most but not all of its impurities. British iron ore normally contains about 94% iron and 6% impurities. The carbon content of steel normally determines its usefulness for specific purposes.

3 A passage with one word missing from each line. The missing word has to be located and identified appropriately.

Example

Matter is name given to everything ______
which weight and occupies space. ______
Matter may exist in states – solid, liquid and gas. ______

4 20 multiple-choice questions testing specialist vocabulary.

Example
Bearing friction can be reduced by using a suitable . . .
solvent resistant irritant lubricant nutrient

Results Successful candidates are awarded endorsements in 3 grades: A, B and C. There are 2 failing grades: D and E.

A successful result in an optional examination at which the candidate is unsuccessful in the main First Certificate examination will be held over by the Syndicate until the candidate qualifies on a later occasion.

Further information As for the main examination (see **17.2**). A specimen paper is also available.

17.7 Literature (Certificate of Proficiency in English)

Title

Conducted by University of Cambridge Local Examinations Syndicate (Cambridge)
Syndicate Buildings, 1 Hills Road, Cambridge CB1 2EU
Tel: Cambridge (0223) 61111

Status An optional additional paper which can be taken only if the candidate has successfully taken or is taking the Certificate of Proficiency in English. It is approved for matriculation purposes by British universities and other institutes.

Aims To provide a qualification in English literature supplementary to the Certificate of Proficiency in English.

Level A special purpose examination at Certificate of Proficiency level (see Appendix 2 for comparative levels of ESP examinations).

Availability As for the main Certificate of Proficiency examination, subject to availability at particular centres (see **17.3**).

Content There is one 3-hour paper with 2 sections. Candidates must answer 2 questions from Section A and 2 from Section B.

Section A consists of passages from the prescribed texts followed by questions.

Section B consists of essay questions with a choice on each text.

Texts are normally prescribed for 2 years and are listed in the Regulations.

Example
Shakespeare (*Julius Caesar*)
Congreve (*The Way of the World*)
Blake (*Songs of Innocence and Experience*)
Charlotte Brontë (*Jane Eyre*)
Shaw (*The Doctor's Dilemma*)
Virginia Woolf (*Mrs Dalloway*)

Kingsley Amis (*Lucky Jim*)
I Bashevis Singer (*A Crown of Feathers*)
Susan Hill (*Strange Meeting*)

Results Successful candidates are awarded endorsements in 3 grades: A, B and C. There are 2 failing grades: D and E.

A successful result in an optional examination at which the candidate is unsuccessful in the main Certificate of Proficiency examination will be held over by the Syndicate until the candidate qualifies on a later occasion.

Further information As for the main examination (see **17.3**). *Information Leaflet 7/44/E (May 1979)* and reports (1965 and 1972) are available.

Title

17.8 Translation (First Certificate, Proficiency and Diploma)

Conducted by University of Cambridge Local Examinations Syndicate (Cambridge)
Syndicate Buildings, 1 Hills Road, Cambridge CB1 2EU
Tel: Cambridge (0223) 61111

Status Translation can be taken as an optional additional paper in the Cambridge examinations in EFL at each of 3 levels – First Certificate, Proficiency, and Diploma. A pass in Proficiency or Diploma Translation is an approved subject for matriculation purposes.

Aims The papers provide a qualification in translation into and from English at the level represented.

Levels The 3 levels offered correspond to the levels of the main examinations (see Appendices 1 and 2).

Availability As for the main examinations, subject to availability at particular centres (see **17.2, 17.3** and **17.4**). The translation test is available only in the languages specified in the Regulations for each year. The languages available in June 1983 were:

First Certificate French, Spanish, Greek, German, Italian, Norwegian, Arabic, Portuguese (for Brazil)
Proficiency French, German, Spanish
Diploma Prior application must be made for all languages at least 5 months before the entry date.

NB: Not all languages are available at all sittings.

Content Two or more passages of varying style will be set for translation both from and into English. The following extracts from the English texts will give some idea of the level and nature of the passages:

First Certificate Level (2½ hours)

It is in clothing and personal accessories that the bulk production of plastics is most important. PVC is now a household word and most people are aware that the light semi-transparent raincoats and the white and leather-finish handbags, which are almost universal, are made of this material, though what it is and how it is made is quite another matter . . .

Certificate of Proficiency Level (3 hours)

Clarke:	I haven't got a white shirt, sir.
Mr Sanderson:	Nonsense, lad. Everybody's got a white shirt.
Clarke:	I've got a white T-shirt with a Mickey Mouse on the front.
Mr Sanderson:	Mickey Mouse on Speech Day! Good God! The end is surely imminent. Robson, you can't possibly go into the hall wearing that leather jacket . . .

Diploma of English Studies Level (Two 3-hour papers, one from and one into English)

Art, in the sense intended here – that is, the generic term subsuming painting, sculpture, architecture, music, dance, literature, drama and film – may be defined as the practice of creating perceptible forms expressive of human feeling. I say 'perceptible' rather than 'sensuous' forms because some works of art are given to imagination rather than to the outward senses . . ..

Results

Successful candidates are awarded endorsements in 3 grades: A, B and C. There are 2 failing grades: D and E.

A successful result in an optional examination at which the candidate is unsuccessful in the main examination will be held over by the Syndicate until the candidate qualifies on a later occasion.

Further information

As for the main examination concerned. *Information Leaflet 7/46/E* is also available.

17.9 English Language (School Certificate and GCE (Overseas Centres))

Title

Conducted by

University of Cambridge Local Examinations Syndicate (Cambridge)
Syndicate Buildings, 1 Hills Road, Cambridge CB1 2EU
Tel: Cambridge (0223) 61111

Status

A joint examination for School Certificate and GCE O level. GCE O level passes are awarded on a single-subject basis. School Certificate is a group examination for which candidates must obtain passes in at least 5 subjects including English Language.

Aims

To assess candidates' ability to read with understanding and to express themselves clearly in writing. In some countries there is also an oral test to assess candidates' ability to express themselves when speaking.

Levels The following table shows the relationship between School Certificate and GCE O level grades:

<table>
<tr><th colspan="2">School Certificate</th><th rowspan="2">GCE O level Grade</th><th rowspan="2"></th></tr>
<tr><th>Standard</th><th>Grade</th></tr>
<tr><td>Very good</td><td>1
2</td><td>A</td><td rowspan="3">Former GCE O level pass standard. (The Pass/Fail concept in the GCE examination has been abandoned.)</td></tr>
<tr><td rowspan="2">Pass with Credit</td><td>3
4</td><td>B</td></tr>
<tr><td>5
6</td><td>C</td></tr>
<tr><td rowspan="2">SC Subject Pass</td><td>7</td><td>D</td><td rowspan="3">Below former GCE O level pass standard. (The Pass/Fail concept in the GCE examination has been abandoned.)</td></tr>
<tr><td>8</td><td>E</td></tr>
<tr><td>Fail</td><td>9</td><td>U= ungraded</td></tr>
</table>

Availability Available only through educational establishments registered as Cambridge examinations centres. Not available to UK centres. The main examination period is November/December but candidates in Malaysia may enter for the examination as a single-subject GCE Ordinary level examination in July. A local paper of similar status and standard but different format is set for candidates in Zambia and is now the responsibility of the Zambian Ministry of Education.

Content Except where there is a third paper testing oral skills, the examination consists of 2 papers.

Paper 1 ($1\frac{1}{2}$ hours)

Marks

1 **Composition** A composition on one of a number of alternative subjects. The subjects may include narrative, descriptive and discussion topics. 50%

Examples

a It is the year 2000. Describe the life you are leading.

b 'Women should be restricted to work connected with the home and children. They should not engage in politics, commerce or industry.' How far do you agree with this statement?

c Write a story about the way in which one person (or you yourself) helped a friend in trouble.

2 Situational composition A composition based on a situation described in detail. No choice of topic.

Example

You are a newspaper reporter and you made the following notes whilst interviewing 3 people who witnessed the fire which destroyed a considerable part of the Zaris Hotel on Independence Avenue. Combining the information from the 3 interviews, write an account suitable for publication in your newspaper.

Elias Mwangi
night watchman – saw smoke from kitchens – time about 3.00 am – raised alarm – joined by night porter – thick smoke – dining room, entrance hall, stairways all impassable – coughing and choking
Mr Christopher Kato
business man from Singapore – woken by shouts and hammering on door – first floor room – grabbed briefcase, shoes, coat – ran into corridor – bad fumes – downstairs to hotel compound
Charles Chang
night porter – woken by smell – met Elias Mwangi – upstairs to warn guests – main staircase now alight – guests on third floor – fire escape available – roused guests shouting 'Fire' – hammered on doors – injured guests – some shocked – called ambulance and fire brigade

Your answer might begin:
'Last night fire destroyed a considerable part of the Zaris Hotel on Independence Avenue. The alarm was given by Elias Mwangi, a night watchman at the hotel, who at about 3.00 am saw smoke pouring from the kitchens. Almost immediately he was joined by the night porter, Charles Chang, who had been woken . . .'
Your account should be approximately 350 words long.

Paper 2 ($1\frac{1}{2}$ hours)

3 Reading comprehension One or more passages of prose upon which open-ended questions are set to test the candidates' ability to understand the content and argument of the text(s) and infer information and meanings. 50%

4 Summary A question based on part or all of one of the reading comprehension passages testing the candidates' ability to summarize.

Results

GCE Certificates are awarded to candidates obtaining grades A–C (1–6). School Certificates are awarded to candidates obtaining grades 1–8 (A–E) in English Language and at least 4 other subjects. School Certificates are generally awarded in 3 Divisions.

Further information

Available from the University of Cambridge Local Examinations Syndicate: Specimen papers; reports on English Language (various years).

18 University of London

18.1 O level English language Syllabus B

Title

Conducted by

University of London School Examinations Department
66–72 Gower Street, London WC1E 6EE
Tel: London (01) 636 8000

Status

A single-subject General Certificate of Education examination for candidates whose mother tongue is not English.

Aims

To provide an examination assessing candidates' competence in using standard written English as a means of communication – free as far as possible from a particularly British or Western cultural context.

Level

A GCE O level examination, equivalent to syllabus A, the examination for candidates in the UK whose first language is English.

Availability

Available only through University of London examination centres overseas or (on request) through centres in the UK. The examination is held twice a year, in January and June. This examination is available from June 1984, when it replaces the O level English Language for Overseas Candidates.

Content

There is one 3-hour paper divided into 3 sections:

Marks

1 **Communication in writing** Two compulsory questions (in which there is some choice of topic) designed to assess a candidate's ability to write effectively in a variety of ways. Narrative, descriptive or discursive topics of a practical nature may be set, and some may require the use of letter form. 40%

Example

Either a Describe, for a visitor, some outstanding feature(s) of your town or country. Write about 200 words.

Or *b* Imagine you are showing a friend a family photograph. Your friend asks what kind of person your brother/sister is. Write what you would say to give a true impression of the character of your brother/sister. Write about 200 words.

2 **Comprehension and summary/directed writing** A prose passage to test a candidate's understanding of written English. A series of comprehension questions requiring both short-form and complete sentence answers, followed by a summary of material from the passage or a piece of directed writing based on it. 40%

Example
In the second paragraph the author describes the characteristics of agricultural life. In a paragraph of about 100 words describe how you think town life differs from the picture of agricultural life which is given in the passage.

3 **English usage** Questions of varying types testing knowledge and understanding of English structures and usage. Types may include modified cloze, sentence rewriting and vocabulary questions. 20%

Results Performance is assessed at 6 grades – A, B, C, D, E and Unclassified (below the minimum level to be recorded). The pass/fail concept has been abandoned at GCE O level but grades A–C correspond to the former subject pass for overseas candidates at GCE O level.

Further information Available from the University of London Publications Office, 52 Gordon Square, London WC1H 0PJ:
GCE Overseas Regulations and Syllabuses
Specimen paper – GCE O level, English Language Syllabus B

Appendices

Appendix 1 Comparative levels of EFL examinations

Approximate Equivalences	Arels Exams Trust	Institute of Linguists		Joint Matriculation Board	Oxford Delegacy of Local Exams
Professional					
Beyond A level	Diploma				
GCE A level ONC/OND BTEC National	Diploma	Grade II Certificate	Examination in EFL – Level 4		
GCE A/O level			Examination in EFL – Level 3	Test in English (overseas)	
GCE O grades A, B, C,	Certificate	Grade I Certificate			Higher level Certificate
BTEC General with credits		Grade I Certificate			
CSE grade 1					
BTEC General Pass					
CSE grade 2					
	Preliminary Certificate				Preliminary Certificate

Pitman Exams Institute		Royal Society of Arts	Trinity College London	University of Cambridge Local Exams Syndicate
			Grade XII Higher Proficiency	Diploma of English Studies
		English as a Foreign Language Stage III	Grade XI Proficiency	Certificate of Proficiency in English
	English Language (NCE) Advanced			
English as a Foreign Lang Advanced	English Language (NCE) Higher Inter			
English as a Foreign Lang Higher Inter	English Language (NCE) Intermediate	English as a Foreign Language Stage II	Grade X Lower Proficiency	First Certificate in English
English as a Foreign Lang Intermediate	English Language (NCE) Elementary	English as a Foreign Language Stage I		Preliminary English Test
English as a Foreign Lang Elementary				

Appendix 2 Comparative levels of ESP examinations

Approximate Equivalences	British Council – ELTS	City & Guilds of London	General Medical Council	Institute of Linguists	London Chamber of Commerce & Industry	
				Final Diploma		
Professional	Band 8		PLAB Test	Final Diploma	Spoken English for Industy & Commerce – Adv	Private & Exec Secretary's Diploma
Beyond A level				Intermediate Diploma		Private Secretary's Certificate
GCE A level ONC/OND BTEC National					SEFIC – Intermediate	
	Band 7					
GCE A/O level	Band 6					Secretarial Studies Certificate
GCE O grades A, B, C,						
BTEC General with credits		Communication in Technical English				
CSE grade 1		Communication in Technical English				
BTEC General Pass	Band 5					
CSE grade 2	Band 4				SEFIC – Preliminary	

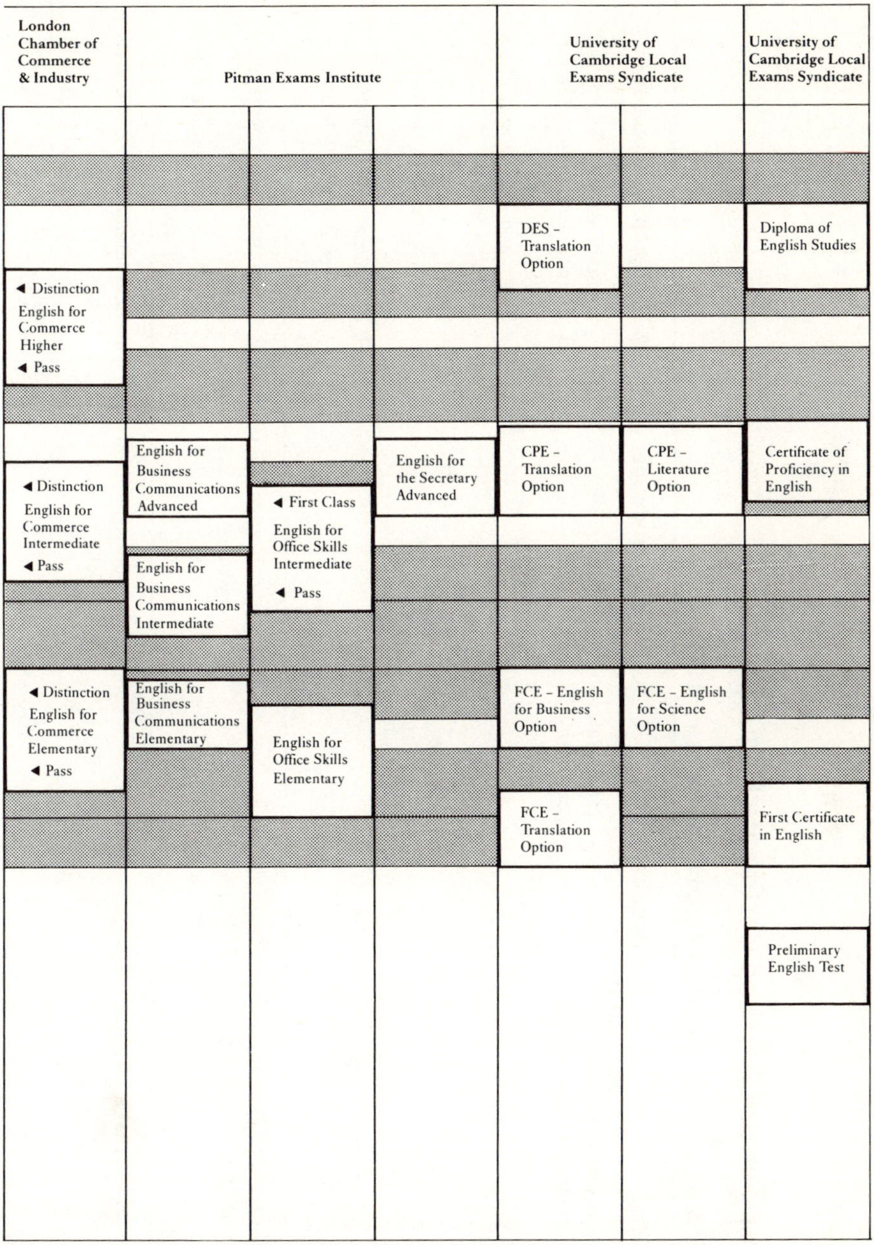
London Chamber of Commerce & Industry
Pitman Exams Institute
University of Cambridge Local Exams Syndicate
University of Cambridge Local Exams Syndicate
DES – Translation Option
Diploma of English Studies
◄ Distinction English for Commerce Higher ◄ Pass
English for Business Communications Advanced
English for the Secretary Advanced
CPE – Translation Option
CPE – Literature Option
Certificate of Proficiency in English
◄ Distinction English for Commerce Intermediate ◄ Pass
◄ First Class English for Office Skills Intermediate ◄ Pass
English for Business Communications Intermediate
◄ Distinction English for Commerce Elementary ◄ Pass
English for Business Communications Elementary
English for Office Skills Elementary
FCE – English for Business Option
FCE – English for Science Option
FCE – Translation Option
First Certificate in English
Preliminary English Test

Appendix 3 Group Certificate Requirements

1 London Chamber of Commerce and Industry (LCCI)

Title	Requirements	English language	All Subjects Compulsory
Private and Executive Secretary's Diploma	6 subjects all at one sitting; 1 may be retaken within 12 months	1 Communication – Use of English	2 Communication – Meetings 3 Communication – Secretarial Skills Shorthand Typewriting Duties: 120/60 wpm *and/or* Audio Typewriting Duties: 60 wpm 4 Secretarial Administration 5 Management Appreciation 6 Interview
Shorthand Typist Diploma	2 subjects	1 Communication – Use of English	2 Communication – Secretarial Skills Shorthand Typewriting Duties: 120/60 wpm
Audio Typist Diploma	2 subjects	1 Communication – Use of English	2 Communication – Secretarial Skills Audio Typewriting Duties: 60 wpm

Private Secretary's Certificate	5 subjects all at one sitting; 1 may be retaken within 12 months	1 Communication – Use of English	2 Communication – Secretarial Skills Shorthand Typewriting Duties: 100/45 wpm *and/or* Audio Typewriting Duties: 45 wpm 3 Structure of Business 4 Office Organization and Secretarial Procedures 5 Interview
Shorthand Typist Certificate (PSC)	2 subjects	1 Communication – Use of English	2 Communication – Secretarial Skills Shorthand Typewriting Duties: 100/45 wpm
Audio Typist Certificate (PSC)	2 subjects	1 Communication – Use of English	2 Communication – Secretarial Skills Audio Typewriting Duties: 45 wpm
Information Processing Certificate (PSC)	3 subjects	1 Communication – Use of English	2 Communication – Secretarial Skills Shorthand Typewriting Duties: 100/45 wpm *and/or* Audio Typewriting Duties: 45 wpm 3 Information Processing

London Chamber of Commerce and Industry (LCCI) cont

Title	Requirements	English language	All Subjects Compulsory
Secretarial Studies Certificate	4 subjects all at one sitting; 1 may be retaken within 12 months	1 Communication – Use of English	2 Communication – Secretarial Skills Shorthand Typewriting Duties: 80/35 wpm *and/or* Audio Typewriting Duties: 35 wpm 3 Background to Business 4 Office Practice
Shorthand Typist Certificate (SSC)	2 subjects	1 Communication – Use of English	2 Communication – Secretarial Skills Shorthand Typewriting Duties: 80/35 wpm

Title	Requirements	English Language	Compulsory Subjects	Other Subjects
Audio Typist Certificate (SSC)	2 subjects	1 Communication – Use of English	2 Communication – Secretarial Skills Audio Typewriting Duties: 35 wpm	

Word Processing Group Certificate (SSC)	3 subjects	1 Communication – Use of English	2 Communication – Secretarial Skills Shorthand Typewriting Duties: 80/35 wpm *and/or* Audio Typewriting Duties: 35 wpm 3 Word Processing	
Elementary Stage Group Certificate Shorthand Typewriting	3 subjects. Distinction in 2, Pass in 3 or Pass in 2 and Distinction in 3	1 English for Commerce (Elementary)	2 Shorthand: 50–60 wpm 3 Typewriting (Elementary)	
Intermediate Stage Group Certificate Shorthand Typewriting	3 subjects as above	1 English for Commerce (Intermediate)	2 Shorthand: 70–100 wpm 3 Typewriting (Intermediate)	
Certificate in Commercial Studies (Elementary)	4 subjects	1 English for Commerce (Elementary)	2 Arithmetic (Elementary)	3 One (Elementary) from: Typewriting; Audio Typewriting; Handwriting 4 One (Elementary) from: Office Practice; Elements of Commerce; Book-keeping

London Chamber of Commerce and Industry (LCCI) cont

Title	Requirements	English Language	Compulsory Subjects	Other Subjects
Business Studies Certificate (Intermediate)	6 subjects. Single subjects counted if obtained over 2 years	1 English for Commerce (Elementary)	2 Book-keeping (Intermediate) 3 Arithmetic (Intermediate) *or* Mathematics (Intermediate) 4 Economics (Intermediate)	5, 6 Two (Intermediate) from: Business Statistics; Commercial Geography; Costing; Mathematics; Structure of Commerce; Typewriting; Shorthand; Languages
Book-keeping Certificate (Intermediate)	3 subjects. Distinction in 1	* See **Other Subjects**	1 Book-keeping (Intermediate) 2 Arithmetic (Intermediate)	3 One (Intermediate) from: English for Commerce; Structure of Commerce
Diploma in Languages (Higher)	3 subjects	* See **Other Subjects**		Three (Higher) from: English for Commerce; French; German; Spanish

2 Pitman Examinations Institute (PEI)

PEI: Basic Commercial Group Certificate	4 subjects all within 12 months	1 One from: English (Elem); English for Office Skills (Elem); English for Business Communications (Elem); English Language (NCE) (Inter); English as a Foreign Language (Higher Inter)	2 Book-keeping and Accounts (Elem) 3 One (Elem) from: Commerce; Office Practice	4 One other PEI subject at Elem or above, excluding Shorthand Theory but including Typewriting Transcription Speed Test (Audio-based)
PEI: Commercial Group Certificate	4 subjects all within 12 months	1 One from: English (Inter); English for Office Skills (Inter); English for Business Communications (Inter); English Language (NCE) (Higher Inter); English as a Foreign Language (Adv)	2 Book-keeping and Accounts (Inter) 3 One (Inter) from: Commerce; Office Practice	4 One from French (Inter); German (Inter); Spanish (Inter); Typewriting (Inter); Audio-Typewriting (Inter 80); Arithmetic (Inter); Understanding Computers (Elem); Keyboarding

Pitman Examinations Institute (PEI) cont

Title	Requirements	English Language	Compulsory Subjects	Other Subjects
PEI: Higher Commercial Group Certificate	5 subjects all within 12 months	1 One from: English (Adv); English for Business Communications (Adv); English for Office Skills (Inter) (First Class)	2 One (Adv) from: Book-keeping and Accounts; Cost and Management Accounts 3 One (Adv) (First Class) from: Commerce; Office Practice	4 One (Inter) (First Class) from: English Language (NCE); French; German; Spanish; Commerce; Cost and Management Accounting (Adv) 5 One from: Typewriting (Inter) (First Class); Audio-Typewriting (Inter 100); Understanding Computers (Elem) *with* Arithmetic (Inter) *or* Keyboarding
PEI: Basic Secretarial Group Certificate	4 subjects all within 12 months	1 One from: English (Elem); English for Office Skills (Elem); English for Business Communications (Elem); English Language (NCE) (Inter); English as a Foreign Language (Higher Inter)	2 Shorthand Speed (60 wpm or more) 3 Typewriting (Elem)	4 One other PEI subject at Elem grade or above, excluding Shorthand Theory Stage I but including Typewriting Transcription Speed Test (Audio-based)

PEI: Secretarial Group Certificate	5 subjects all within 12 months	1 One from: English (Inter); English for Office Skills (Inter); English for Business Communications (Inter); English Language (NCE) (Higher Inter); English as a Foreign Language (Adv)	2 One from: Shorthand-Typewriting (Inter 100); Shorthand Speed (100 wpm) *and* 20 wpm in Typewriting Transcription Speed Test (Shorthand based) 3 Typewriting (Inter) 4 Secretarial Practice (Inter)	5 One (Inter) from: Book-keeping and Accounts; French; German; Spanish; Commerce; Audio-Typewriting (Inter 80); Word Processing (Theory and Practice); Systematic Note-taking
PEI: Higher Secretarial Group Certificate	5 subjects all within 12 months	1 One from: English (Adv); English for Office Skills (Inter) (First Class); English for Business Communications (Adv); English for the Secretary (Adv); English for Office Skills (Inter) *and* Word Processing – (Theory and Practice)	2 One from: Shorthand-Typewriting (Adv 120); Shorthand Speed (120 wpm) *and* 22 wpm in Typewriting Transcription Speed Test (Shorthand based) 3 Typewriting (Adv) 4 Secretarial Practice (Adv)	5 One from: Audio Typewriting (Inter 100); Commerce (Inter); Book-keeping and Accounts (Inter) (First Class); French (Inter) (First Class); German (Inter) (First Class); Spanish (Inter) (First Class); English Language (NCE) (Adv) (First Class)

Appendix 4 Teacher training courses in English as a Foreign/Second Language

1 **Academic courses in Britain**

There are courses available at universities, polytechnics and colleges of education. Diploma courses usually run from October to June and masters courses for 12 months from October. Diploma courses usually require the minimum of a teaching qualification and/or a degree and experience in teaching EFL/ESL. A good degree plus relevant teaching experience is usually required on a course leading to a master's qualification.

Short refresher courses, usually held during the summer, are available at some institutes.

Details of academic courses are available from the British Council.

2 **Royal Society of Arts Examinations Board**

The RSA offers 6 schemes for teaching English as a second or foreign language:

a *Diploma in the Teaching of English as a Foreign Language to Adults* for those teaching adult foreigners in further education establishments and private language schools (usually known as the Further Education Scheme). Available in UK or overseas. Intended for experienced teachers who are native English speakers.

b *Preparatory Certificate for the Teaching of English as a Foreign Language to Adults* for those without previous experience in teaching adult foreigners, and for practising teachers with no previous training in EFL. Available in the UK and overseas.

c *Diploma in the Teaching of English as a Second Language in Multi-Cultural Schools* for those qualified teachers teaching English as a second language to primary and secondary children in multi-cultural schools (usually known as the Primary and Secondary Scheme). Available in the UK and Australia.

d *Diploma in the Teaching of English as a Second Language in Further, Adult or Community Education* for those teaching English to adult immigrants. Candidates should have a standard of spoken and written English which will make them acceptable to students from the ethnic groups they are likely to encounter. Available in the UK and Australia.

e *Certificate in Initial Training* (*TESL*) for those involved in ESL in a professional or voluntary capacity. Available in the UK only. Candidates should have a standard of English acceptable to students from a variety of ethnic groups which they will encounter.

f *Diploma for Overseas Teachers of English* designed for those whose native language is not English who are teaching English overseas. Available only overseas. Candidates should have at least the standard of English required to pass RSA Stage II EFL.

Further details may be obtained from:
The Royal Society of Arts Examinations Board
John Adam Street, Adelphi, London WC2N 6EZ
Tel: London (01) 839 1691

3 **Trinity College London**

a *Preliminary Certificate in Teaching English as a Foreign Language,* designed as initial training for those with a British degree or teaching certificate (or equivalent). Trinity College validates courses conducted at certain institutions in UK and overseas.

b *Licentiate Diploma for Teachers of English as a Foreign or Second Language,* designed for practising teachers of EFL/ESL with at least 2 years' experience. The Diploma is open to both native and non-native speakers. Non-native speakers must have a standard of English equivalent to that required to pass Trinity College Grade 12 Spoken English or Cambridge Proficiency. Available in the UK and certain overseas countries.

Note: A revised syllabus for the Licentiate Diploma is to be introduced in January 1985.

Full details of syllabuses, regulations and centres offering tuition for the schemes are available from:
Trinity College London
11–13 Mandeville Place, London W1M 6AQ
Tel: London (01) 935 5773

4 **English Speaking Board (International) Ltd**

Diploma of the English Speaking Board in the Teaching of English as an Acquired Language, designed for experienced teachers in the field of teaching English as an acquired language. The standard of written English required is that equivalent to the post-graduate certificate of education. Open to native and non-native speakers. Available in the UK only, except by special arrangement.

Further details may be obtained from:
English Speaking Board (International) Ltd
32 Roe Lane, Southport, Merseyside PR9 9EA
Tel: Southport (0704) 34587

5 **The College of Preceptors**

Teaching of English as a Second Language Options available as part of the Diplomas of Associate, Licentiate (University first degree level) and Fellow of the College of Preceptors. Designed for experienced teachers (trained teachers may claim certain exemptions), UK and overseas.

Further details may be obtained from:
The College of Preceptors
Coppice Row, Theydon Bois, Epping, Essex CM16 7DN
Tel: Theydon Bois (037 881) 2727

Appendix 5 Addresses of Professional Bodies offering English Language Examinations

The Association of International Accountants Ltd
Turvey Abbey
Turvey, Bedfordshire MK43 8DE
Tel: Turvey (023064) 471

The Association of Legal Secretaries
The Mill
Clymping Street
Clymping, Sussex BN17 5RN
Tel: Littlehampton (090 64) 3710

British Society of Commerce Ltd
25 Bridgeman Terrace
Wigan WN1 1TD
Tel: Wigan (0942) 43572

Chartered Insurance Institute
CII Administrative Office
31 Hillcrest Road
London E18 2JP
Tel: London (01) 989 8464

Deutscher Volkshochschul-Verband EV
Padagogische Arbeitsstelle
Holzhausenstrasse 21
6 Frankfurt/Main,
West Germany
Tel: 59 09 88

Faculty of Teachers in Commerce Ltd
141 Bedford Road
Sutton Coldfield
West Midlands B75 6DB
Tel: Birmingham (021) 378 1265

Institute of Administrative Accounting and Data Processing
Walter House, 418–422 Strand
London WC2R 0PW
Tel: London (01) 240 3106

Institute of Chartered Secretaries and Administrators
16 Park Crescent
London W1N 4AH
Tel: London (01) 580 4741

Appendix 6 Addresses of Overseas Examining Bodies

Caribbean Examinations Council
The Garrison
St Michael 20
Barbados, West Indies

Department of Technical Education and Vocational Training
PB RW 16
Lusaka, Zambia

The East African Examinations Council
PO Box 7066
Kampala, Uganda
and
PO Box 73598
Nairobi, Kenya

Hong Kong Examinations Authority
Canton Road Government Offices
393 Canton Road, 11th floor
Kowloon, Hong Kong

Vocational and Industrial Training Board
Vocational Drive
Singapore 0513

The West African Examinations Council
Headquarters Office
Private Post Bag
Accra, Ghana

Glossary and abbreviations

Achievement Test See **Attainment**

A Level Advanced level examination of the General Certificate of Education (see GCE).

Argument Used to describe written composition in which different points of view are presented (see **Discussion**).

Attainment/Achievement Test A test based on a given area of knowledge specified in a syllabus, course of study, etc. (This definition does not apply to ELTDU's use of **Attainment** – see **6.1**.)

Aural Comprehension (also **Audial**) Understanding of spoken language rather than written.

Authentic Text Any piece of language which is written or spoken for purposes other than language teaching.

Battery A number of tests where each question tests one particular aspect of language, eg comparatives. There are usually a large number of questions.

BTEC Business and Technician Education Council.

Case Study Collected information on a particular situation with details of all the circumstances involved.

Cloze Used to describe a test of written language where a number of words are missed out in a text, usually at regular intervals, for example, every fifth word. Candidates have to put in the missing words. This is said to measure reading comprehension. See **Modified Cloze.**

Communicatively Used to describe the use of language in a situation where information is exchanged, either in speech or writing; usually contrasted with the use of language in the classroom when language is used to show a knowledge of its grammar (see **Usage**).

Connected Writing/Continuous Prose Sentences forming a paragraph or a series of paragraphs; not isolated sentences which are unconnected.

Controlled Response An answer for which the candidate has been given help in the form of notes, words, etc. See **Free Response**.

CSE Certificate of Secondary Education, the level that is expected of the average 16-year old student in Britain.

Cued-conversation A conversation where the candidate is asked specific questions.

Data Facts or information.

Diagnostic Test A test to find a candidate's particular strengths and weaknesses (see **Profile**).

Dialogue A spoken or written conversation between 2 or more people.

Dictation A test where a passage or separate sentences or words are read aloud by the examiner for the candidate to write down exactly what is said.

Directed Questioning Questions used to elicit a particular response to test vocabulary, grammar, etc.

Discursive Used to describe a written composition presenting a reasoned argument. See **Argument**.

Discussion Used to describe either a spoken conversation in which the speakers share ideas, or a written composition in which different points of view are presented.

EFL (English as a Foreign Language) Used to describe the English learned by non-native speakers where English is not used as a lingua franca, eg a German native speaker learning English in Germany would be described as an EFL learner. EFL is usually contrasted with ESL (English as a Second Language) which is English used by non-native speakers as a lingua franca, eg a Hindi native speaker living in Britain would use English as a second language.

Elicit To get a response, either spoken or written.

ESL See EFL.

ESP (English for Special/Specific Purposes) Used to describe the English used in particular circumstances, eg for banking, for medicine, for flying, etc.

Expository Usually used to describe a written text which explains or gives information.

Format The style and arrangement of an examination paper, book, etc.

Free Response An answer or reply to a question where no help is given with what to say or write. See **Multiple Choice, Objective Test, Open Completion.**

Free Writing An answer, usually a composition, where the candidate is given no help (see **Guided Composition**).

Functions A classification of language by what it is used for rather than by grammar, eg apologizing, greeting, complaining, etc. See **Usage**.

GCE General Certificate of Education, the examinations designed for academically-inclined students in British secondary schools. GCE is held at 2 principal levels: O (Ordinary) level, designed for 16-year olds; and A (Advanced) level, designed for 18-year olds. A levels are usually required for admission to universities or other institutions of higher education.

Guided Composition Used to describe written work where candidates are given part of the composition in the form of notes or incomplete sentences or pictures etc, which they must use to produce a complete answer.

Interlocutor A person (usually a teacher) with whom a candidate holds a conversation during an oral test. The candidate's performance in the conversation is assessed by the examiner.

Intonation The way the voice goes up and down in speaking.

Item One question in an examination.

Master's Course/Qualification A university course leading to the postgraduate degree of Master of Arts, Master of Science or Master of Education.

Medium A means of using language; usually written or spoken.

Modes Mode 1: both the syllabus and the examination are written by the board. Mode 2: the syllabus is written by the teachers but the examination is written by the board. Mode 3: both the syllabus and the examination are written by the teachers, but are validated by the board (see in particular 15.1).

Modified Cloze Describes tests in which words are missed out in a written text according to what the examiner wants to test, eg all structure words are deleted. Also the test may be presented in different ways, eg there may be no spaces to indicate where a word has been left out, or multiple choice answers may be given for each missing word. See **Cloze**.

Multiple Choice A question which gives the candidate a choice of answers, only one of which is the right answer.

Narrative Used to describe a written composition which tells a story, usually in the first person.

Narrative Padding Sentences in a text giving descriptive background to a sequence of events or narrative.

Objective Question/Test A test in which the questions demand only one right answer, usually given in the form of multiple choice items. See **Multiple Choice**.

O Level Ordinary level examination in the General Certificate of Education (see **GCE**).

ONC/OND Ordinary National Certificate/Diploma.

Open Completion/Open Ended Used to describe questions which give part of the answer but leave the candidate to finish it without any help other than the part given.

Optional Open to choice, not compulsory.

Productive Skills Language skills shown by the candidates producing language either spoken or written rather than the skills of reading or listening. See **Receptive Skills**.

Professional Level An examination for someone who has undergone advanced education and special training in a particular occupation.

Proficiency Test A test to measure a candidate's language ability at the time of testing regardless of the courses he has done or qualifications he holds.

Profile Used to describe examination results which give individual marks for each part of the examination showing areas of strength and weakness, rather than giving one mark for the whole examination. Such results can be used diagnostically (see **Diagnostic Test**).

Receptive Skills The language skills of listening and reading. See **Productive Skills**.

Register The kind of language used in particular circumstances, eg legal, medical, formal/informal language, etc.

Role Play When a candidate is expected to act as though he is someone else, eg a tourist, an angry person, etc.

Root Word A word or part of a word on which all other forms of that word are based, eg act is the root word of actor and acting.

Series/Session Used to describe the time examinations are sat, eg summer, spring and winter series.

Short-Form Question An examination question in which there are one or 2 words missing from a sentence. The candidate must write in any suitable words to complete the sentence. A series of such sentences would form a **Cloze** text.

Situational Conversation A dialogue based on given material, eg a picture, a described state of affairs.

Social English The language used in informal, everyday situations, eg meeting people.

Structure Grammar.

Sustained Speaking Talking over a period of time without stopping.

Syntax Grammar.

Threshold Level A specification of a level of language proficiency drawn up for the Council for Cultural Co-operation of the Council of Europe. The level described is that required for people to be able to communicate socially on straightforward everyday matters, to be able to get around and lead a reasonably normal social life when visiting another country. See **Waystage, Unit-Credit Examination**.

Typographical Error A mistake made in typed or printed material.

ULCI Union of Lancashire and Cheshire Institutes, incorporated in the North Western Regional Advisory Council for Further Education.

Unit-Credit Examination A system of examinations which divides the syllabus into portions (**Units**). Candidates can be examined in some or all units at a sitting. **Credit** is then given for all the units successfully attempted. Units which candidates fail can be retaken at a later date. The term was first introduced by the Council of Europe and the system is becoming more widely adopted in English language examinations.

Usage The grammar of the language. See **Communicatively**.

Visual Stimuli Pictures, graphs, diagrams, etc,. not text, used to elicit language.

Waystage A specification of a level of language proficiency below Threshold Level for modern language learning for adults. See **Threshold Level, Unit-Credit Examination**.